LILIAN'S KITCHEN

HOME COOKED FOOD

by Lilian Hiw

LILIAN'S KITCHEN

www.lilianskitchen.co.uk
Bringing a Taste of Asia to You

SINGAPORE

THAILAND

VIETNAM

INDIA

KOREA

MALAYSIA

CHICKEN SATAY	30
CHICKPEA CURRY	32
CURRY PUFFS	34
PINEAPPLE PEANUT SAUCE	36

INDONESIA

BEEF RENDANG	40
GADO GADO SALAD	42
PERFECT FLUFFY RICE	44
YOUNG CORN SATAY	46

HONG KONG

CHILLI OIL PORK DUMPLINGS	70
CHINESE FIVE SPICE WONTONS	72
PORK SIEW MAI	74
SESAME PRAWN TOAST	76

CHINA

BEEF IN BLACK BEAN SAUCE	80
GARLIC PAK CHOY	82
GOLDEN EGG FRIED RICE	84
KUNG PAO PRAWNS	86

JAPAN

BEEF GYOZA	110
CITRUS PONZU DIP	112
SMOKED SALMON NIGIRI BALLS	114
TERIYAKI SALMON	116

TREATS

LEMONGRASS MOJITOS	120
MANGO LASSI	122
MANGO STICKY RICE	124
MISO TOFFEE PINEAPPLE	126
SEXY WOBBLE PANNA COTTA	128
LILIAN'S SINGAPORE SLING	130

Hello from Lilian

Thank you for the privilege of sharing with you my experiences, and the cuisine of my heritage and my part of the world. I have included recipes that are comforting and can be cooked often at home, some that are easy and quick for weekdays, and some that are more indulgent, show-stopping recipes that will impress friends at a dinner party.

My aim is to demystify Asian cooking, making traditional dishes more approachable and less complicated, and using readily available ingredients to achieve that authentic taste.

To make sure that the recipes were fool proof, I asked friends from different walks of life to try out these recipes. I chose friends of different genders and ages, from novice cooks to professional chefs. The feedback I asked for included their experience of getting the ingredients, whether my logic made sense, whether my sequence and methods were easy to understand and follow, etc. I also asked them to include a photo of their finished dish, so that I could judge whether the recipe produced the desired end product. I am so blessed to have such great friends to trust with this important task.

I wanted to share more than just recipes with you, so I have included lots of advice, tips, and trade secrets that I have picked up over my 40 plus years in the food and catering industry.

Cooking Clock

The Cooking Clock is a brilliant concept to organise your ingredients and cooking sequence. Lay out the ingredients on a plate or tray, the ingredient that is cooked first will be positioned at 12 o'clock, the rest of the ingredients follow according to the length of time they will take to cook. For example, any root vegetables will be positioned at an earlier time (say 3 o'clock) than green leafy vegetables (say 6 o'clock), and any herbs or garnishes will be placed in the last position at 11 o'clock. Try it out for any cuisine, it is especially useful for quick stir frying as time is of the essence in the presence of a hot wok.

Food Allergies

Peanuts are a common ingredient in many Asian dishes. We use peanut butter in some of the recipes in this book. If you have a peanut allergy, you can substitute it with peanut-free butter, such as 'Wow Butter', which is made from toasted soya. Alternatively, if you are NOT allergic to other nuts, you can replace the peanut butter with cashew or almond butter.

Super Crunchy

The secret to super crunchy fried chicken is in the double frying technique - the first fry releases the fat from the chicken skin, the resting allows the chicken to redistribute its juices through the meat, and the second fry locks in the crispness. It can stay crisp for a couple of hours.

Wok's Breath

Heat control! You will be rewarded with what the Chinese call 'wok's breath', the lovely smoky flavour and aroma of stir-fried dishes from restaurant kitchens and street vendors. Heat your pan to smoking point before you add oil (which should have a high smoke point, such as vegetable oil), then heat the oil until it is hot and swirl it around the pan. This will also help prevent food from sticking to the pan. A non-stick pan is not suitable because the non-stick coating does not tolerate high heat. Domestic hobs don't usually give off enough heat, so the trick is to keep portions small and cook in batches. It is easy to achieve once you learn the tips and techniques.

Sushi Texture

Sushi is best when eaten on the day it is made. Although it can be kept in the fridge for a day or two, the rice will become chalky. Do not make pieces of sushi to be eaten the next day. Store any excess rice in a covered container in the fridge. Reheat it the next day and the rice will be soft and fluffy again; cool the rice and you can then make your sushi.

Gluten Free and Vegetarian

Lee Kum Kee offers a fair selection of gluten free and vegetarian sauces, such as mushroom vegetarian stir-fry sauce and gluten free hoisin, soy and oyster sauces.

Tasting

If you are making a large batch of food that will be sealed before cooking, such as dumplings, spring rolls or curry puffs, etc. Cook a teaspoon of the filling to taste test. Adjust any seasoning before assembling the whole batch.

Customise

I would suggest that you follow the recipes exactly the first time. Then make a note of your personal preferences, such as the level of spiciness, or how sweet or salty you like your food, to suit your taste buds, and make adjustments for future cooking.

Freezing Ginger

Frozen ginger is easier to grate, has a smoother texture and is less fibrous. To freeze ginger, peel and cut the fresh ginger into thumbnail size pieces and seal in a freezer bag or covered container. Remove the quantity you need and grate from frozen.

The secret to juicy and succulent lean meat

The fat in meat imparts flavour, contributes to its juiciness and texture, however some of us might prefer the leaner cuts of meat for health reasons, or simply do not like the texture of fat in our mouth. But if not handled properly, learn meat can taste dry, like a piece of cardboard!

The strategy?

Marinating impart flavour and add moisture. Low temperatures and long cooking times allow the meat to cook slowly without drying out. Resting helps to redistribute the juices throughout the meat. But there is one ingredient that can be added to improve texture, give a more satisfying mouth feel and keep your lean meat tender and juicy.

Read on for more nuggets of information and I hope that you will love this cookbook as much as I do.

Happy Cooking!

Growing Up In Singapore

My parents had a food stall selling pig intestine congee and fried noodles in Princess market. This was my first apprenticeship in food and customer service.

Singapore is a culturally diverse city - you can find food from all over the world on this tiny island. There is a cuisine for every taste and budget, and we talk about what we are going to eat for the next two meals while eating the first! You can't help but love food when you're surrounded by so many passionate foodies!

My Humble Beginnings

Our old kitchen at home was tiny, and my grandmother used to chase me out of it all the time. My curiosity and the desire to cook grew, so I enrolled myself in a catering school to learn about classic cooking from the basics. I did my apprenticeship in numerous 5-star hotels, where I was trained to cook different cuisines. I fell in love with everything that the hospitality industry has to offer. I have worked in both Front and Back of House, Sales & Marketing, and Training. When you're having so much fun, it's not work anymore.

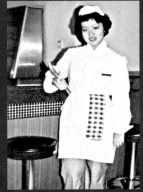

1980

Hotel & Catering
Training School
Singapore

1984

L'Ecole Hoteliere
De Lausanne
SHATEC Singapore

1987

SHATEC
Training Officer
Singapore

1991

Raffles Hotel
Singapore

1994

West Suffolk Colle e
Lecturer UK

1995

Degree in
Adult Education
UK

1998

Tung Lok Restaurant
Group Vice President
Singapore

2001

Kayu Furniture
Managing Director
UK

My Wonderful Family

I met my husband Jon while buying a mattress. He personally delivered it to my house and the rest, as they say, is history! We're celebrating our 20th wedding anniversary this year.

Our son Daniel is our pride and joy, a wonderful young man. He has a gift in the kitchen with good taste buds and natural cooking skills. We enjoy cooking together as a family. They are such blessings in my life and I love them so much.

... And Now

I had Daniel when I was 41 years old. As a more mature mother, I felt that it was important to teach him life skills early on so that he would be well equipped to look after himself in the future. I dedicated 10 years to Daniel and took a career break to be a full-time mum and homemaker, working part-time from home selling cakes. Twelve years later, at the age of 53, I found myself at a career crossroads. Should I continue with my last job in furniture retail, or return to my first love - food? I followed my passion and started Lilian's Kitchen.

2009

Proprietor UK

2017 until now

Chef / Owner

Private Chef-Bespoke Dining

I take my guests on a culinary journey, travelling through Asia from the comfort of their own dining room! They can choose where they want to go: perhaps cocktails from Singapore, some canapés from Vietnam, Hong Kong, or Indonesia? A trip to Thailand, Malaysia, or India for the main course, maybe a fusion dessert? I don't just cook and serve their food, I like to share background stories, or some cooking tips if they like to cook.

I pride myself on taking care of every detail and pampering everyone so that the hosts can relax and enjoy themselves.

Private Cooking Lesson

It could be for a couple wanting to spend quality time together, or for a family reunion or a team building event. I also offer a mini masterclass followed by a bespoke dinner. Every occasion is different. I've developed some recipes for Lifeplus, based on their health food products, and they sent a film crew to film the cooking and it has gone global. It is all very exciting!

Cookery School

It's a privilege to share the food of my heritage and my part of the world. It gives me great pleasure to see my students blossom and produce amazing authentic tasting food that they can cook again and again at home. I love seeing all the photos they send me or when they tag me on my social media platforms. We have a saying: 'Arrive as a guest, leave as a friend and return as family'. I feel honoured that so many family members return to my classes.

Bespoke Cakes

I baked for 12 years when I took a career break to look after my son. I used to make character cakes, fondant cakes and themed cakes. I have gradually found my style and what I love most - contemporary cake art designs using buttercream, tempered chocolate and stained-glass rice paper!

Community & Media

Giving back to the community is important, as is the sharing of knowledge and culture. I've done demonstrations for food festivals, multicultural and WI groups to share tips on Asian cooking. It was also wonderful to be invited by Simply Good Food TV to be part of their '24 hours of cooking' and I'll never forget cooking live on stage at the Bury St Edmunds Theatre Royal to celebrate their 100th anniversary. I've been blessed to appear in major publications - both press and magazine - and on local and national radio shows. Never a dull moment, I love it!

My Food Columns

I was delighted to be invited by the Bury Free Press to write a monthly food column. It goes out to various press publications and online in the Suffolk News. At first I was intimidated by the thought of producing a double page spread every month, but as I have developed as a food writer I am now really enjoying the experience.

新加坡 SINGAPORE

LILIAN'S DRUNKEN BEEF NOODLES

Serves: 2 - 3

Prep time: 10 minutes

Cook time: 20 minutes

INGREDIENTS

Beef marinade

200g sirloin, fillet
or rump steak

½ tsp sea salt

½ tsp ground
white pepper

1 tsp cornflour

Sauce

1 tbsp light soy sauce

1 tbsp dark soy sauce

1 tsp brown sugar

1 tsp sesame oil

2 tbsp Shaoxing
rice wine

4 tbsp water

Stir fry ingredients

2 tbsp vegetable oil

400g fresh egg noodles

100g fresh bean sprouts

100g pak choy,
5cm lengths

The name was inspired by the very spicy Thai "drunken noodles" dish, where legend has it that a husband woke his wife up in the wee hours of the morning, after a very drunken night, and demanded that she cook him some noodles. She added loads of chilli to punish him. My dish is made "drunk" by adding real alcohol – Shaoxing rice wine, delicious!

METHOD

1. **Marinate beef:** Trim off any fat and sinew. Cut the meat against the grain, into thin slices, about 4cm by 1cm. With the flat side of your knife, tenderise the beef by 'smacking' it. Mix with the other beef marinade ingredients.

2. **Sauce:** Combine all the sauce ingredients in a bowl. Stir and set aside.

3. **Cook:** Heat the wok until smoking, then add the oil. Seal the beef for 1 minute, taking care not to cook it through. Set aside to rest.

4. Heat the wok again, add the oil and fry the noodles until it has charred bits and smells fragrant and smoky. Smoke in batches if your pan is small or the heat is weak.

5. Add the bean sprouts, greens and sauce. Return the beef to the wok, toss to combine.

6. **Serve.**

CHEF'S TIPS

1. Replace with dry sherry if you really can't get Shaoxing wine for this dish, as the fragrance is different. Shaoxing wine is readily available in major supermarkets and online.
2. It is important to heat the wok until it is very hot and continue to cook at a high temperature to achieve a smoky flavour.

MUM'S SWEET & SOUR PORK

Serves: 2 - 3

Prep time: 15 minutes

Cook time: 25 minutes

INGREDIENTS

Pork marinade

400g pork shoulder, 3cm cubes

2cm cube ginger

1 large shallot

2 large garlic cloves

1 tsp sea salt

½ tsp ground white pepper

6 tbsp cornflour

3 tbsp water

Sauce (see chef's tips)

2 tsp cornflour

1 tbsp castor sugar

1 tbsp rice or cider vinegar

1 tbsp light soy sauce

8 tbsp water

Stir fry Ingredients

500ml vegetable oil, for deep frying

1 medium onion, diced same size as the pork

2 tbsp tomato paste

1 small red bell pepper, diced same size as the pork

80g pineapple chunks, tinned or fresh

Serving suggestions

Fluffy rice (page 44)

Garlic pak choy (page 82)

Originating from the Canton region of China, the sauce started as a simple vinegar and sugar mixture. Chefs then used hawthorn berries and preserved plums to add colour to the sauce. Later, Hong Kong chefs used ketchup and Worcestershire sauce to mark their blend. My mum used ketchup to colour hers. I have tweaked it a little and used tomato paste as I like the deeper red colour and the depth of flavour it gives.

METHOD

1. **Marinate:** Grate or pound the ginger, shallot and garlic to a fine pulp, squeeze 2 tsp of juice from the pulp into a large bowl and discard the pulp. Add all the 'pork marinade' ingredients to the bowl. Marinate for 10 minutes.

2. **Sauce:** Combine the ingredients in a separate bowl and set aside.

3. **Deep-fry:** Fill a wok or deep saucepan half full with oil, heat on a medium high heat to 180°C. Test by putting the handle of a wooden spoon into the oil, when bubbles gather around the handle the oil is hot enough. Place the pork into the oil with tongs, easing the food into the oil away from you to avoid being splashed. Cook a small batch at a time to prevent the pork from sticking together. Do not touch it for the first 2 minutes to allow a 'crust' to form before flipping it over. Fry until golden brown, about 6 to 7 minutes. Drain on a kitchen towel.

4. **Stir-fry:** Heat 1 tbsp of the oil (from the deep frying) in a wok or frying pan over a medium heat. Fry the onion until soft but still firm, add the tomato paste and roast it for 30 seconds to intensify the flavour and colour. Add the pepper, pineapple and sauce, stir and simmer for 1 minute. Adjust the seasoning to your taste.

5. **Serve:** Add the pork to the sauce, stir to coat evenly and serve immediately.

CHEF'S TIPS

1. The marinade imparts flavour and helps to tenderise the pork.
2. Pork shoulder has some fat running through it. You can use diced lean pork instead, as the cornflour in the marinade will lock the moisture in the pork.
3. The amount of sauce is designed to just coat the pork, if you prefer more sauce, double the recipe.

PERANAKAN CHICKEN CURRY

Serves: 4

Prep time: 20 minutes

Cook time: 35 minutes

INGREDIENTS

Spice paste

5 medium fresh
red chilies

8 shallots

5 garlic cloves

3cm length fresh
ginger, skinned

3cm length fresh turmeric
or 1 tbsp ground turmeric

1 tsp shrimp paste
or 1 tsp fish sauce

1 tbsp water

Curry

1 kg chicken thighs

200g white
waxy potatoes

5 tbsp vegetable oil

400ml coconut milk

200ml water

2 tsp sea salt

1 tsp castor sugar

1 small cinnamon bark

1 star anise

2 stalks fresh
lemongrass, crushed

6 frozen Makrut Thai
lime leaves

Serve

Fluffy rice (page 44)

The term Peranakan generally refers to a person of mixed Chinese and Malay or Indonesian heritage, descendants of early Chinese migrant traders who married local Malay women. A female Peranakan is known as Nonya and a male Peranakan is known as a Baba. Peranakan or Nonya cuisine is a fine hybrid of Chinese and Malay flavours, using an abundance of ingredients, flavours and techniques from both cultures. True fusion food that will excite your taste buds.

METHOD

1. **Prep:** Blitz all the spice paste ingredients in a food processor until smooth. For a less spicy curry, scrape out the seeds from the chillies. For a more spicy curry, use chilli padi, also known as bird's eye chilli.

2. Cut the chicken thighs in half. Peel the potatoes and cut into 3cm chunks. Soak the potatoes in a bowl of water.

3. **Cook:** Heat the oil in a wok or saucepan on a medium heat, fry the spice mix until some oil floats to the surface. Add all the 'curry' ingredients except the lime leaves, stir well and simmer for 25 minutes. Stir occasionally until the chicken and potatoes are cooked through, add the lime leaves.

4. **Serve.**

CHEF'S TIPS

You can use deboned and skinned chicken thighs, but the bone and skin do impart a depth of flavour.

ROTI JOHN [ASIAN 'BURGER']

Serves: 2

Prep time: 5 minutes

Cook time: 10 minutes

INGREDIENTS

2 eggs

1 tsp chilli sambal or chilli powder

1 small baguette

1 tsp vegetable oil

100g minced lamb

½ tsp sea salt

1 small onion, chopped

Serving suggestions

Cucumber slices

Tomato slices

Mayonnaise

Ketchup

Roti means bread in Malay. 'Roti John' first appeared in the 1960s; when an English serviceman stationed in Singapore asked an Indian hawker (street food vendor) for a hamburger. Having no hamburger to offer, the hawker had the clever idea to make use of whatever ingredients he had at his food stall at the time to create one. He fried up some minced mutton and onions with eggs and tucked them into a small loaf. All those years ago, the locals could not speak English, so all Caucasian men were addressed as "John". After the dish was cooked, the hawker shouted for 'John' to pick up his 'Roti', thus the birth of the legendary Asian 'burger' - Roti John.

METHOD

1. **Prep:** Whisk the eggs with the chilli in a bowl and set aside.

2. Slice the baguette in half lengthwise, do not slice through the bread, keep one half connected to the other.

3. **Cook:** Heat the oil in a frying pan, cook the lamb on a medium high heat until brown. Season with the salt.

4. Pour the egg mixture into the lamb and give it a stir. Cook the mixture until the eggs are almost set on the bottom but still moist on top. Add the onions.

5. Open the baguette and place the cut side down onto the lamb and egg mixture, tuck any overflowing mix under the baguette and press the bread down firmly with a spatula to glue the mix and bread together. Cook for another minute until golden brown.

6. Flip the baguette over carefully to brown the other side. Fold the two halves back together and cut the baguette into 4 pieces.

7. **Serve:** Drizzle the Roti John with the mayonnaise and ketchup. Place the sliced cucumber and tomatoes next to the Roti John.

CHEF'S TIPS

You can add grated cheese for a fusion twist!

马来西亚 MALAYSIA

CHICKEN SATAY

Makes: 25 to 30 skewers

Prep time: 15 minutes

Cook time: 10 minutes

INGREDIENTS

500g chicken breast
or thigh

2 tsp caster sugar

½ tsp ground
white pepper

1 tsp sea salt

1 tsp ground coriander

1 tsp ground turmeric

1 tsp garlic powder

1 tsp cornflour

2 tsp vegetable oil
(plus more for grilling)

Short bamboo skewers

Serve

Cucumber and red onion,
cut into 2cm cubes.

Peanut sauce (page 36)

These grilled meat skewers originated from Indonesia, inspired by the kebabs from the Middle East and India. Spelt 'sate' in Indonesia and 'satay' in Singapore and Malaysia, they refer to the same dish. Interestingly, in the Hokkien dialect, satay sounds like 'sa-tae' which translates to 'three pieces'. The satay in Singapore and Malaysia tend to have three pieces of meat on the skewer, while in Indonesia and Thailand they have more.

METHOD

1. **Prep:** Soak the bamboo skewers in cold tap water for 10 minutes.

2. Cut the chicken roughly into 2cm x 1cm pieces. Combine with all the other ingredients and mix well. Thread 3 pieces of chicken onto each skewer.

3. **Cook:** Brush the chicken with oil then grill on a barbecue or under an overhead grill on a high heat. Cook for 1 minute on each side, until both sides are slightly charred and cooked through.

4. **Serve:** The diced cucumber and red onions add freshness. We poke them onto the chicken skewer, then dip them in the peanut sauce, and eat them all in one mouthful. Try it, it's good!

CHEF'S TIPS

Soaking the skewers reduces the chances of them burning over an open grill. If cooking under an overhead grill, cover the exposed bamboo skewers with a strip of aluminium foil.

CHICKPEA CURRY

Serves: 4 as a side dish

Prep time: 5 minutes

Cook time: 15 minutes

INGREDIENTS

1 tsp ground cumin

1 tsp ground coriander

1 tsp ground turmeric

2 tbsp vegetable oil

1 medium onion, chopped

3 garlic cloves, chopped

100ml passata
(sieved tomatoes)

1 tin of chickpeas,
drained weight 240g

100ml water

1 tsp salt

½ tsp garam masala

1 tbsp fresh coriander,
roughly chopped

Serving suggestions

No fuss flatbread
(page 92)

Fluffy rice (page 44)

Chickpeas tick so many boxes. They are rich in plant protein, high in fibre, low in fat, a rich source of vitamins and minerals, and great for gluten free, vegan and vegetarian dishes. My son discovered the wonders of chickpeas thanks to this recipe.

METHOD

1. **Prep:** Mix the ground cumin, coriander and turmeric with 2 tablespoons of cold tap water to form a paste.

2. **Cook:** Heat the oil in a saucepan over a medium heat. Add the chopped onions and garlic and cook for 2 minutes until brown.

3. Add the spice paste and fry until it looks glossy and some oil oozes out, stirring constantly.

4. Stir in 2 tablespoons of the passata and cook out the spices for a further 2 minutes, stirring constantly.

5. Add in the drained chickpeas, the rest of the passata, water and salt, simmer for 5 minutes.

6. **Serve:** Add the chopped coriander and garam masala, stir and serve.

CHEF'S TIPS

Mixing the ground spices with water to form a paste will protect the spices from getting burnt when frying.

CURRY PUFFS

Makes: 17

Prep time: 15 minutes

Cook time: 20 minutes

INGREDIENTS

200g potatoes
(2 medium)

2 tbsp curry powder
mixed with 2 tbsp water

1 small red onion, finely
chopped

2 garlic cloves, finely
chopped

1 tbsp vegetable oil

2 tbsp coconut milk,
Chaokoh or Aroy-D brand

3 tbsp frozen peas

3 tbsp plain flour, for
rolling

1 ready rolled short
pastry (320g)

1 egg, beaten

1 litre vegetable oil, for
deep frying (or you
can bake)

Inspired by various 'mini pies' like the British Cornish pasty, Portuguese empanada and Indian samosa during the colonial era, the traditional Malay style curry puff uses an oil dough wrapped in a flour dough, turned and folded many times to create lamination and a flaky finish. We will use ready rolled short pastry and it tastes equally delicious!

METHOD

1. **Prep:** Peel and cut the potatoes into quarters, cook in a pan of water with 1 tsp of salt until cooked (roughly 12 to 15 minutes). Pierce the potatoes with a small knife, if the knife goes through without resistance, it is cooked. Drain, mash and set aside. Mix the curry powder with the water and set aside in a bowl.

2. **Filling:** Heat the oil, fry the onion and garlic for 2 minutes on a medium heat. Add the curry paste, fry for 2 more minutes. Then add the coconut milk and fry for another 2 minutes. Add the peas and potatoes, mix well. Cool.

3. **Assemble:** Dust the work surface with flour and unroll the pastry. Punch out 17 discs with a 7.5cm cookie cutter. Cover with a damp cloth to keep the pastry from drying out. Moisten the edge of the pastry with the egg. Place a heaped teaspoon of the filling in the middle of the pastry, fold in half pushing out any air pockets and seal tightly. Crimp the edge to make it look pretty.

4. **Deep fry:** Fill a wok or deep saucepan half full with oil, heat to 180°C. Test by placing the handle of a wooden spoon into the oil, when bubbles gather around the handle the oil is hot enough. Lower the puffs into the oil with a slotted spoon to avoid being splashed. Fry a handful at a time, overcrowding lowers the temperature of the oil and the pastry will absorb the cool oil and get greasy. Turn to ensure even browning, transfer to paper towels to drain.

5. **Or bake:** Alternatively, after point 3, prick the pastry with a fork and brush with the beaten egg; bake at 180°C for 20 - 25 minutes until golden brown.

PINEAPPLE PEANUT SAUCE

Serves: 6

Prep time: 5 minutes

Cook time: 15 minutes

INGREDIENTS

Spice paste

2 tbsp water

1 tsp ground coriander

1 tsp ground turmeric

1 tsp chilli powder

Sauce

2 tbsp vegetable oil

1 small onion, finely chopped

2 garlic cloves, crushed

200ml coconut milk, Chaokoh or Aroy-D brand

3 level tbsp smooth peanut butter

2 tbsp grated pineapple (grate the flesh not the core)

200ml water

1 tsp caster sugar

1 tsp sea salt

Serve

Crushed roasted salted peanuts

Chicken satay (page 30)

This is perhaps better known as satay sauce to some, as this delicious sauce is most commonly served as a dip with satay. Being neighbours, Singapore and Malaysia uses very similar ingredients, flavours and culinary styles. The only difference in this Malaysian peanut sauce is the addition of grated pineapple, giving it a lovely fragrance and a sweet and sour finish.

METHOD

1. **Prep:** Mix the spices with the water to form a paste. Set aside.

2. **Cook:** Heat the oil in a saucepan over a high heat, fry the onions for 2 minutes until fragrant. Add the garlic and continue to fry until lightly brown.

3. Turn down the heat and fry the spice paste for 2 minutes, then add 2 tablespoons of the coconut milk and continue to fry on low heat until the spice mixture looks glossy and some oil seeps out (2 - 3 minutes). Add the rest of the ingredients, bring to a boil then simmer, stirring frequently, for 10 minutes until some oil floats to the surface.

4. **Serve:** Sprinkled with some crushed peanuts.

CHEF'S TIPS

The trick to preventing the ground spices from burning and becoming bitter, is to mix them with water to make a moist paste.

INDONESIA

BEEF RENDANG

Serves: 2 - 3

Prep time: 20 minutes

Cook time: 1 hr 40 minutes

INGREDIENTS

1 kg chuck steak

5 tbsp vegetable oil

4 cloves, garlic

4 star anise

4 green cardamom, cracked

5cm cinnamon stick

2 tsp tamarind puree

2 tsp sugar

2 tsp salt

350ml coconut cream

200ml water

6 Makrut lime leaves, sliced

Spice paste

6 shallots

6 garlic cloves

4cm fresh ginger

6 cashews

4 lemongrass stalks

2 fresh red chillies

10 dried long chillies

Kerisik

6 tbsp desiccated coconut

Serve

Fluffy rice (page 44)

Beef rendang is a 'dry' curry with a reduced thick sauce, and has an incredible depth of flavour with many layers of spices. It's actually straight forward to make, it just requires some time, and patience.

METHOD

1. **Prep:** Blend the spice paste ingredients in a food processor to a fine paste. Trim away any sinews from the beef, cut into 4cm cubes.

2. **Cook:** Heat the oil in a heavy based pot, fry the spice paste until it looks shiny. Add the beef, fry for 2 minutes, then add the rest of the ingredients. Cover and simmer for 1 hour, stirring occasionally. After the hour, remove the lid and simmer for 30 minutes to reduce the sauce, stirring frequently. The sauce might look pale and runny, but the oil will separate from the sauce towards the last 10 minutes. The beef will start to fry in this oil, turn brown and the sauce will thicken.

3. If the meat is a little tough after 1 ½ hours, add a few spoons of water and simmer until it is tender. If the meat is tender before the sauce is reduced to the desired thickness, move the meat to a bowl, and boil the sauce rapidly until it is thickened. Stir constantly.

4. Toast the desiccated coconut in a dry frying pan until it turns brown, then pound to a paste with a pestle and mortar. Stir into the curry.

5. **Serve.**

CHEF'S TIPS

Choose a beef cut with connective tissues, it'll give that tender melt-in-the-mouth sensation.

GADO GADO

Serves: 2

Prep time: 10 minutes

Cook time: 15 minutes

INGREDIENTS

Dressing

1 tbsp light brown sugar

1 tbsp fish sauce

2 tbsp fresh lime juice
(1 lime)

2 tbsp smooth peanut
butter

4 tbsp coconut milk,
Chaokoh or Aroy-D brand

1 garlic clove

1 small fresh red chilli

Salad

100g beansprouts

100g green beans

2 eggs

4 waxy new potatoes

200g firm tofu

1 tbsp vegetable oil

½ cucumber

Serve

Prawn crackers

Gado is an Indonesian word for 'mix'. A medley of raw and blanched vegetables, with protein of hard boiled eggs and fried tofu, and something crunchy like prawn or emping crackers. Arranged beautifully on a plate, and served with a peanut sauce. You can whisk up this light no-cook peanut dressing, or make a peanut sauce (see chef's tips). Create a potpourri with your favourite seasonal vegetables, or use what is in the fridge, and enjoy your own 'mix mix' salad!

METHOD

1. **Dressing:** Deseed the chilli for a less spicy dressing. Place all the ingredients in a small food processor (or use a hand blender), and blitz until smooth.

2. **Cook:** Bring a pan of water to the boil, add 1 tsp of salt. Blanch the beansprouts for 30 seconds, remove to a bowl of cold water with a perforated spoon. Cool, drain and place on a serving plate.

3. Add the beans to the pan and boil for 1 - 2 minutes until tender, refresh in cold water, drain and place on the serving plate.

4. Cut the new potatoes in halve. Boil the eggs and potatoes in the same pan for 9 minutes. Remove the eggs and peel under water starting from the base (it's easier). Slice in half and arrange on the serving plate.

5. Pierce the potatoes with a small knife, if you get resistance, boil for another few minutes and check again. Cool, cut into slices and arrange on the serving plate.

6. Dry the tofu with some kitchen paper towel, cut into cubes and panfry with a tablespoon of vegetable oil until crispy. Add to the serving plate.

7. **Serve:** Cut the cucumber into slices or dices, dot it around on the serving plate. Drizzle over the peanut dressing, and serve with the prawn crackers.

CHEF'S TIPS

1. Other vegetable suggestions - cabbage, spinach, tomatoes, radish, carrots.

2. If you're using the cooked peanut sauce recipe on page 36 omit the pineapple and add 2 tbsp of lime juice.

PERFECT FLUFFY RICE

Serves: 2

Soak time: 10 minutes

Cook time: 12 - 15 minutes

INGREDIENTS

150g uncooked rice, Jasmine or Basmati

260ml water

There are different methods of cooking rice, this is an absorption method. The measured water is absorbed by the rice, resulting in fluffy and separated grains of rice. The water measurement in this recipe is for Jasmine and Basmati rice, different types of rice will have different cooking times and water requirements.

METHOD

1. **Wash the rice:** Gently swish the rice grains in the cooking pot with your hands, the water will turn a milky white colour. Tip out the cloudy water, carefully catching any escaping rice grains with your hands. Add fresh water, swish the rice again. Drain the washed rice in a sieve to remove all the water.

2. **Soak:** Leave the rice in the pot with the 260ml of water for 10 minutes to soak.

3. **Cook:** By any of the following methods:

   - Microwave rice cooker - Cook on high for 12 minutes, rest the cooked rice in the sealed pot for 2 minutes.

   - Rice cooker - Depending on their features and functions, different rice cookers can take different amounts of time to cook rice (check the manufacturer's instructions for cooking times). My rice cooker is a single function model and takes 15 minutes to cook rice, including the resting time.

   - Stove-top - Bring the rice to a boil over a high heat, stir once. Reduce the heat to the lowest setting and cover with the lid. Simmer for 9 – 10 minutes or until the water is fully absorbed. Remove from the heat, and rest the rice for 2 minutes.

CHEF'S TIPS

1. If you prefer to measure by using a cup instead of weighing, the ratio is 1 cup of rice to 1 ¾ cups of water.
2. 1 cup of uncooked rice will yield two cups of cooked rice, which can serve 2 main course portions.

YOUNG CORN SATAY

Serves: 2

Prep time: 5 minutes

Cook time: 10 minutes

INGREDIENTS

1 packet baby/young corn (around 8)

Sauce

3 tbsp brown sugar

2 tbsp light soy sauce

2 garlic cloves, roughly chopped

2cm cube fresh ginger, skin on, roughly chopped

2 star anise

2 cloves

Chargrilled and brushed with kecap manis, this is so easy yet so delicious. Kecap manis is a thick and dark molasses-like sauce made from simmering dark sugar and soy sauce with aromatic spices. The word manis means sweet, so the sauce is often referred to as sweet soy sauce too.

You can buy a bottle of kecap manis, or make your own with this recipe. It is such a versatile sauce - use it in Asian-style salad dressings, Indonesian satay, peanut sauces, grilled chicken, pork, beef, fish and seafood. It is the primary sauce used in Indonesia's national dish of nasi goreng (fried rice). My son uses it as a dip and even drizzles it over his pasta.

METHOD

1. Place all the ingredients for the sauce in a small saucepan, bring to a boil and simmer for 30 seconds. Set aside to infuse.

2. Wash and dry the baby corn, grill on a high heat until you get nice char marks on the corn but it should still be firm.

3. Brush with the sauce and continue to grill for another minute until it is sticky and brown on all sides.

4. Lovely as a snack or as a side vegetable dish to a roast or barbecue.

CHEF'S TIPS

1. You can pan-fry instead of grilling.
2. If you like to buy a bottle of Kecap manis, I would recommend the Indonesian brand ABC.

泰国 THAILAND

MANGO SOM TUM

Serves: 4 side portions

Prep time: 15 minutes

INGREDIENTS

1 large garlic clove,
peeled

1 Thai bird's eye chilli
or a less spicy
chilli variety

2 tbsp palm sugar
or light brown sugar

4 fine green beans, cut
into 3cm lengths

4 cherry tomatoes,
halved

1 large green mango,
peeled

2 tbsp lime juice (1 lime)

2 tbsp fish sauce

4 tbsp toasted peanuts,
lightly crushed

In the Thai language, Som means sour taste and Tum means pounding. This is a refreshing pounded salad using a wooden pestle and clay mortar to crush the ingredients releasing their aromas. The art is to have a light hand when pounding so that the ingredients don't get smashed and still retains its crunch. The craggy edges also help cling on to and absorb the dressing. Generally, people associate green papaya with som tum salad. However, the locals do use other crunchy fruits or vegetables so I am using green mangoes for this recipe. Cucumber is another popular choice (use only the flesh and not the inner core of watery seeds).

METHOD

1. Pound the garlic and chilli to a chunky paste in the pestle and mortar. Grind in the palm sugar on the side of the mortar.

2. Pound the green beans and smash the tomatoes gently.

3. Add the lime juice and fish sauce.

4. Cut the flesh of the mango into fine strips, add to the mortar.

5. Combine all the ingredients, holding a spoon in one hand while lightly pounding with the pestle in the other hand. Taste and adjust the seasoning, balancing the sweet, sour, spicy and salty. Sprinkle over the peanuts, give it a final mix and serve immediately.

CHEF'S TIPS

Use a wooden bowl and the flat end of a wooden rolling pin in place of the som tum pestle and mortar.

PAD THAI SALAD

Serves: 4

Prep time: 25 minutes

INGREDIENTS

Dressing

2 tbsp castor sugar

1 tbsp fish sauce

2 tbsp light soy sauce

3 tbsp toasted sesame oil

4 tbsp fresh lime juice and zest (about 2 limes)

2 garlic cloves, finely chopped

1 fresh red chilli, finely chopped

Salad

50g dried glass noodles (see chef's tips)

2 large carrots

2 large courgettes

2 spring onions, sliced

1 handful fresh coriander, chopped

1 handful fresh mint leaves, chopped

2 handfuls roasted peanuts, chopped

Inspired by the flavours of Pad Thai noodles, I made this salad one hot summer's day and fell in love with the bold and refreshing flavours.

METHOD

1. Measure all the ingredients for the dressing into a jar, cover and shake until the sugar is dissolved.

2. Soak the noodles in boiling water for 2 minutes, rinse in cold tap water and drain. Snip the noodles into 10cm lengths with a pair of scissors and place in a large serving bowl.

3. Peel and cut off the top and tail of the carrots and courgettes. Use a spiraliser or julienne peeler to cut into thin long strips, add to the bowl.

4. Sprinkle the herbs and peanuts over the vegetables.

5. Toss the salad lightly with the dressing just prior to serving.

CHEF'S TIPS

1. Glass noodles are also known as mung bean vermicelli, cellophane or bean thread noodles, and are gluten free.
2. When grating the lime for its zest, grate only the outer green layer, the white pith underneath is bitter.

PRAWN PAD THAI NOODLES

Serves: 2

Prep time: 10 minutes

Cook time: 20 minutes

INGREDIENTS

3 tbsp vegetable oil

180g raw king prawns, deveined

3 garlic cloves, chopped

180g dried flat rice noodles, 5mm thick

2 eggs, beaten

80g beansprouts

20g spring onions, cut to 4cm lengths

Sauce

1 tbsp light brown sugar

1 ½ tbsp fish sauce

1 tbsp oyster sauce

2 tsp tamarind puree, seedless

2 tsp dark soy sauce

Serve

Lime wedges

Crushed chilli flakes

Salted peanuts

Raw beansprouts

Spring onions

This chewy stir-fried noodle dish is delicious, balancing sweet, sour and savoury notes. High heat is essential to ensure that the noodles cook quickly and evenly. The heat from a domestic hob is less intense compared to that of a street food vendor or restaurant. I would recommend using a large frying pan or wok to cook small batches of noodles at a time to give them enough space to fry. Overcrowding the pan will result in soggy noodles, and a risk of the noodles sticking to the pan.

METHOD

1. **Prep:** Soak the dried noodles in boiled water for 5 minutes. Rinse with cold tap water and drain.

2. Combine all the sauce ingredients in a bowl.

3. **Cook:** Heat the pan until smoking, add 1 tbsp of the oil to coat the pan. Add the prawns and fry until they turn pink. Do not overcook the prawns as they will become rubbery. Set aside on a plate.

4. Drizzle 1 tbsp of the oil in the pan, fry the garlic until lightly brown, being careful not to burn it. Quickly add the noodles, fry over a high heat, tossing the noodles lightly with a pair of chopsticks in one hand and a wooden spoon in the other. Pour over the sauce and mix well.

5. Push the noodles to one side of the wok, drizzle the rest of the oil into the empty space, add and scramble the eggs.

6. Add in the beansprouts, spring onions, prawns and peanuts, toss to mix.

7. **Serve:** With lime wedges, crushed chilli flakes, salted peanuts, raw beansprouts and spring onions, placed on the side of the plate.

CHEF'S TIPS

Tamarind paste can be found in major supermarkets, Asian supermarkets and online. At a push, ketchup has been used as a replacement with reasonable success.

THAI GREEN CURRY CHICKEN

Serves: 4

Prep time: 15 minutes

Cook time: 15 minutes

INGREDIENTS

500g chicken breast, 3cm cubes

1 tsp sea salt

1 tbsp cornflour

400ml coconut milk, Chaokoh or Aroy-D brand

50g green curry paste, Mae Ploy brand

100g aubergine, diced

100g red bell peppers, diced

100g bamboo shoots, sliced

100g green beans, 3cm lengths

300ml water

6 Makrut Thai lime leaves

10g Thai sweet basil leaves

10g fresh coriander, chopped

1 tbsp light brown sugar

1 tbsp fish sauce

Serve

Fluffy rice (page 44)

There is no shame in using a shop-bought curry paste, just make sure you get an authentic brand! The ingredients had been basking in the tropical sun, picked at its peak, their best flavours captured and nurtured by local expertise. When you open the packaging, Thailand jumps out at you! Just a word of caution though, don't follow the packet instruction, just use half the quantity and go from there or you might have your head blown off!

METHOD

1. **Prep:** Marinate the chicken with the salt and cornflour, set aside. Cut the vegetables into 2cm cubes.

2. **Cook:** Add 4 tablespoons of the creamy part of the coconut milk to a hot pan, stirring frequently until it splits and some oil floats to the top. Lower the heat, add the curry paste and fry until fragrant.

3. Add the aubergine and 150ml of water, simmer for 2 - 3 minutes until it is cooked but still firm to the touch.

4. Add the chicken, vegetables and the rest of the coconut milk and water, simmer for 10 minutes until they are cooked and tender.

5. Remove the stalks from the lime leaves and slice finely, add to the curry with the other herbs. Adjust the seasoning with sugar and fish sauce. This is a sweet and spicy curry.

CHEF'S TIPS

1. It is important to get a good quality coconut milk that has a good proportion of fat to coconut water, and tastes pure. If you struggle to get one of the listed brands, replace 150ml of the water with coconut cream.

2. The cornflour keeps the chicken breast moist and tender.

越南 VIETNAM

FRESH SUMMER ROLLS

Makes: 8 Rolls

Prep time: 25 minutes

A great DIY party food! They are so easy to make, your guest can create their own rolls and customise with their favourite ingredients laid out on the table. These are gluten free too!

INGREDIENTS

8 sheets of rice paper wrappers

16 large cooked fresh prawns, deveined

100g dried rice vermicelli

100g iceberg lettuce, sliced

50g fresh beansprouts

1 carrot, cut into fine strips

Handful of fresh mint leaves

Handful of fresh coriander leaves with stalks

Serving suggestions

Nuoc cham sauce (page 62)

Hoisin peanut dip (page 62)

METHOD

1. **Prep:** Soak the vermicelli in boiling water for 2 minutes, rinse in cold water, drain and place in a pile on a tray. Place all the other ingredients in separate heaps on the same tray.

2. **Assemble:** Fill a large bowl with room temperature water. Immerse the rice paper for 20 seconds, remove and place on a plate. Do not soak the rice paper for too long or it will turn soft and floppy, and be difficult to handle.

3. Place your filling in the centre, towards the bottom corner closest to you. Don't overfill, as this can make the rolls difficult to fold. Lift the bottom corner of the wrapper up and over the filling, tucking it under slightly to hold the filling in place. Fold the left and right corners towards the middle, over the filling, so that they meet or overlap. Continue to roll the wrapper away from you, keeping it tight around the filling. Repeat until all the summer rolls have been made.

4. **Serve:** With nuoc cham sauce or hoisin peanut dip.

NUOC CHAM SAUCE

Makes: Roughly 300ml

Prep time: 10 minutes

INGREDIENTS

250ml water

2 tbsp castor sugar

3 tbsp fish sauce

2 tbsp lime juice and zest, from 1 lime

1 tsp rice or cider vinegar

1 large fresh red chilli, finely chopped

2 cloves fresh garlic, finely chopped

The principle sauce used in any Vietnamese kitchen as a dip, a sauce or marinade. Some people refer to it as nuoc mam; nuoc cham translates as 'dipping sauce' while nuoc mam means 'fish sauce'. It is quick and easy to make and will keep for a week in the fridge.

METHOD

1. Measure all the ingredients into a jar, secure tightly and shake until the sugar is completely dissolved.

CHEF'S TIPS

If you prefer your sauce less spicy, use a spoon to scrape out the seeds and the white woody membrane from the inside of the chilli before chopping it.

HOISIN PEANUT DIP

Makes: Roughly 100ml

Prep time: 5 minutes

INGREDIENTS

2 tbsp creamy peanut butter

2 tbsp hoisin sauce

2 tbsp boiled water, to thin down the sauce

1 tsp sriracha chilli sauce

1 tsp light soy sauce

1 tsp fresh lemon juice

1 tsp salted peanuts, crushed

No cooking is required, this dipping sauce can be whipped up in minutes! A handy recipe that tastes great with just about anything!

METHOD

1. Measure all the ingredients into a jar, shake well and serve with the crushed peanuts.

CHEF'S TIPS

A great "make ahead" sauce that will keep for a couple of weeks in an air tight container. Use a clean dry spoon each time to scoop out the sauce.

LEMONGRASS PORK SKEWERS

Makes: 6 skewers

Prep time: 10 minutes

Cook time: 15 minutes

INGREDIENTS

For the pork skewers

500g pork mince, 12% fat

½ tsp ground black pepper

½ tsp sea salt

½ tsp caster sugar

2 tbsp fish sauce

2 garlic cloves, finely chopped

1 large shallots, finely chopped

6 stalks lemongrass

Serve

Nuoc cham sauce (page 62)

1 large baguette, divide into 6 pieces

12 iceberg or gem lettuce leaves

Handful of fresh mint leaves

Handful of fresh coriander

I like using stalks of fresh lemongrass as the skewers for this dish – they look beautiful and infuse the pork with their citrus aroma and flavour. You can use thick bamboo or metal skewers instead, and add finely chopped fresh lemongrass to the pork for the flavour and fragrance.

METHOD

1. **Filling:** Combine all the ingredients for the pork skewers, except the lemongrass, in a bowl and mix well with your hands working up a 'elasticity' in the meat, this will give the meat a 'bouncy' texture.

2. **Assemble:** Peel off the tough outer layer of the lemongrass, trim off any brown bits at both ends of the lemongrass. Crush the bulb end of the lemongrass lightly with the back of your knife to expose the fragrance. Divide the mixture into 6 portions, mould the meat around the bulb end of the lemongrass to cover one third of the length of the lemongrass. Shape it like a sausage. Repeat until all 6 are done.

3. **Cook:** Grill or panfry on a medium high heat until golden brown and cooked through.

4. **Serve:** Slice the baguette in half lengthwise, do not slice through. Place 2 lettuce leaves, some herbs and the pork in between the bread. Remove the lemongrass stalk from the meat before eating with some nuoc cham sauce.

CHEF'S TIPS

If you prefer to use a lower fat content meat, add 2 teaspoons of cornflour to the filling mixture to keep the meat moist.

VIETNAMESE SPRING ROLLS

Makes: 12 spring rolls

Prep time: 15 minutes

Cook time: 20 minutes

INGREDIENTS

12 Vietnamese
rice paper

200ml vegetable oil
for shallow frying

Filling

300g minced pork,
12% fat

100g white crab meat
or chopped raw prawns

200g glass noodles (also
known as mung bean
vermicelli/cellophane
noodles)

30g black fungus

100g carrots, coarsely
grated

2 large garlic clove,
grated

2 large shallot, grated

1 tbsp fish sauce

1 tsp sea salt

1 tsp ground white
pepper

Serve

Iceberg or gem lettuce

Fresh mint leaves

Fresh coriander

Nuoc cham sauce
(page 62)

These spring roll wrappers are made from rice flour and filled with noodles, seafood, meat and vegetables - it's almost a complete meal in one bite! They are eaten dipped in a sweet, sour and spicy dip, then wrapped in a lettuce leaf with lots of fresh herbs added to it. Very refreshing and delicious.

METHOD

1. **Prep:** Soak the glass noodles in hot water for 2 minutes, rinse in cold water, drain then cut into 3cm length. Soak the black fungus in hot water for 2 minutes, wash off any grit trapped in the folds of the fungus. Drain, cut into 3cm length and mix with all the 'filling ingredients' in a bowl.

2. **Assemble:** Immerse a piece of rice paper in a wide bowl half filled with room temperature water for a mere 3 seconds, remove and place on a clean dry teacloth.

3. Place the filling in the centre, towards the bottom corner closest to you. Don't overfill, as this can make the rolls difficult to fold and cause it to burst when frying. Lift the bottom corner of the wrapper up and over the filling, tucking it under slightly to hold the filling in place. Fold the left and right corners towards the middle, over the filling, so that they meet or overlap. Continue to roll the wrapper away from you, keeping it tight around the filling. Repeat until all the spring rolls have been made.

4. **Cook:** Heat the oil in a shallow frying pan to a medium heat. Place the spring rolls in the pan, it is important to leave some space between them, so that they do not stick together. Fry both sides until crispy, about 7 minutes. (It will not turn golden brown like the Chinese style spring rolls). Transfer to a cooling rack placed over a baking tray to drain excess oil. Do not use paper towel as it might stick to the spring rolls.

5. **Serve:** Encase the spring roll in a fresh lettuce leaf and herbs of your choice, serve with nuoc cham sauce.

CHEF'S TIPS

1. Do not soak the rice paper for too long, it will turn soft and be difficult to handle. Too much moisture will also cause spitting during frying.
2. Use silicon tongs or two wooden spoons to fry. The warmed rice paper is soft and sticky, and will cling on to cold metal tongs making holes in the spring rolls.

香港 # HONG KONG

CHILLI OIL PORK DUMPLINGS

Makes: 32 to 39

Prep time: 20 minutes

Cook time: 20 minutes

INGREDIENTS

1 pkt gyoza wrappers, defrosted

Filling

500g minced pork, 12% fat

10g fresh coriander, choped

40g spring onion, finely sliced (about four stalks)

½ tsp sea salt

1 tsp ground white pepper

2 tsp toasted sesame oil

2 tsp light soy sauce

Chilli oil

2 tbsp chilli flakes

1 tbsp ground chilli

2 tbsp white sesame seeds

½ tsp sea salt

150g vegetable oil

1 cinnamon bark, 5cm

1 shallot, sliced

2 spring onion, sliced

Serving suggestions

A dash of Chinese black vinegar or Balsamic vinegar

A drizzle of sesame oil

Make your own chilli oil with this recipe, it is really quick and easy to make. But if you're short on time, you can also pick up a jar of chilli oil, they are readily available in the shops, very convenient and so delicious and authentic. There are many brands out there, my favourite is 'Lao Gan Ma crispy chilli in oil'

METHOD

1. **Chilli oil:** Toast the white sesame seeds in a dry pan until lightly golden. Add to a deep heat-proof bowl with the chilli flakes, ground chilli and salt. Add the cinnamon, shallots, spring onions and oil to a saucepan, heat the oil over medium low heat. Fry for 4-5 minutes until golden brown. Strain the hot oil through a metal sieve into the bowl of the chilli mix, stir and set aside to serve.

2. **Filling:** Combine all the ingredients for the filling in a bowl and mix thoroughly. Cook a teaspoon of the filling to check and adjust the seasoning before assembling the whole batch.

3. **Make dumplings:** Place a teaspoon of filling onto the middle of a wrapper, moisten the edge with water. Fold the wrapper over to form a half moon sealing the contents without trapping any air inside. Crimp 5 pleats along the edge of the dumpling. Repeat until all the wrappers have been used.

4. **Cook:** Boil the dumplings in water until they float to the surface (2 - 3 minutes). Remove with a slotted spoon.

5. **Serve:** Toss in some chilli oil.

CHEF'S TIPS

Make the chilli oil in advance if you can, it'll taste even more amazing left to infuse overnight. It'll keep for a couple of weeks stored in an airtight jar. Remember to use a clean dry spoon each time you scoop out some chilli oil.

CHINESE FIVE SPICE WONTONS

Makes: 32 to 39

Prep time: 20 minutes

Cook time: 20 minutes

INGREDIENTS

1 packet wonton wrappers, defrosted (32 to 39 sheets, depending on the brand)

1 litre vegetable oil, for deep frying

Filling

500g minced Pork, 12% fat

10g fresh coriander, chopped

100g water chestnuts, tin. Cut into small cubes

½ tsp sea salt

½ tsp ground white pepper

1 tsp Chinese five spice powder

2 tsp toasted sesame oil

2 tsp light soy sauce

Serve

Chilli sauce

Traditionally these dumplings were served in a clear broth and they look like floating clouds. The name "wonton" translates as "swallowing clouds" in the Cantonese dialect. Wontons can also be served 'dry' by cooking them in water, then draining and serving them tossed in a sauce like oyster sauce or chilli oil. Or they can be deep-fried, which is the method chosen for this recipe.

METHOD

1. **Filling:** Mix all the ingredients for the filling in a bowl. Cook a teaspoon of the filling to check and adjust the seasoning before assembling the whole batch.

2. **Make wontons:** Place a tablespoon of the filling onto a wrapper, moisten the edge with water, fold the wrapper in half to make a rectangle shape. Pinch the wrapper together to make it look pretty. Repeat.

3. **Fry:** Fill a wok or deep saucepan half full with the oil, heat on medium to 180°C. Place the handle of a wooden spoon into the oil, when bubbles gather around the handle the oil is hot enough for frying. Lower the wontons into the oil with a slotted spoon, placing the food into the oil away from you to avoid being splashed. Fry only a handful at a time as overcrowding would lower the oil temperature and the pastry might get soggy and greasy. Turn occasionally to ensure even browning, cook until golden brown, about 6 minutes.

4. Transfer to some paper towels to drain off excess oil.

CHEF'S TIPS

1. If you're using lean pork, add 2 teaspoons of cornflour to the mixture. It will keep the meat moist.
2. Wontons taste best freshly cooked. If you are cooking ahead of time, keep the wontons warm in an oven at 80°C, covered loosely with some foil. Do not seal with the foil to avoid condensation and soggy wontons.
3. Wontons freeze well for 2 months. Cook them from frozen, for a slightly longer time and ensure that the filling is piping hot before serving.

PORK SIEW MAI

Makes: 32 - 39

Prep time: 20 minutes

Cook time: 8 minutes
(9 minutes from frozen)

INGREDIENTS

1 packet wonton
wrappers, defrosted
(32-39, depending
on brand)

Filling

500g minced pork,
12% fat

200g fresh raw prawns

100g water chestnuts,
cut into small cubes

½ tsp sea salt

½ tsp ground white
pepper

2 tsp toasted sesame oil

2 tsp light soy sauce

1 tsp Chinese rice wine or
dry sherry

1 egg

Garnish (optional)

On top of the siew
mai - little carrot dices,
fresh coriander leaves,
peas or fish roe

Serving suggestions

Chilli sauce

Chilli oil (page 70)

Siew Mai is one of the classic trio of dishes that are popular and a must-eat when one dines at a dim sum restaurant. Dim sum literally translates to 'touch the heart' in Cantonese. Legend has it that the Royal Chefs of the Imperial Court, many centuries ago, created intricate little delicacies to delight the palette and 'touch the heart' of the Chinese Emperors and the royal family. Make these open top dumplings to touch the heart of your family and friends!

METHOD

1. **Prepare the steamer basket:** Cut out a round disc of parchment paper to fit the bamboo steamer, cut a few holes about 5mm in diameter randomly in the paper, or use a hole puncher. Brush the paper with some vegetable oil.

2. **Prepare the filling:** Mix all the ingredients for the filling in a bowl. Cook a teaspoon of the filling to check and adjust the seasoning before assembling the whole batch.

3. **To assemble:** Trim the corners off the square wonton wrappers to get round wrappers. Place a heaped dessert spoon of the mixture in the middle of each wrapper, draw up the sides of the wrapper. Wrap your fingers and thumb (like making a fist) around the dumpling, squeeze the wrapper into the meat firmly so that the filling sticks well to the wrapper. Push the meat down from the top with the other thumb so that the filling meets the edge of the wrapper, leaving the top exposed.

4. **Cook the dumplings:** Place the siew mai into the steamer basket, spaced slightly apart. Fit the basket over a pan of boiling water, ensuring a tight fit, cover with the lid. Steam the siew mai for 8 - 9 minutes (or 9 - 10 minutes from frozen). Push a small knife through the middle of a siew mai and if clear liquid oozes out it is cooked.

5. **Serve:** Directly from the bamboo steamer underlined with a plate, with your favourite chilli sauce.

CHEF'S TIPS

1. The egg helps to bind, and retain moisture in the meat.
2. Freeze the siew mai uncooked. Cook them 'on demand' from frozen whenever you fancy some. Check that it is cooked before serving.

SESAME PRAWN TOAST

Makes: 32 pieces

Prep time: 15 minutes

Cook time: 15 minutes

INGREDIENTS

8 slices thin white sandwich bread

100g white untoasted sesame seeds

500ml vegetable oil, for frying

Prawn paste

500g raw prawns, chopped

100g, minced pork, 12% fat

50g water chestnut, chopped

3 tbsp spring onion, sliced

½ tsp sea salt

1 tsp caster sugar

½ tsp ground white pepper

1 tsp cornflour

2 tsp sesame oil

1 tbsp light soy sauce

1 egg

Serve

Chilli sauce

The ingredients list might look long but I promise that this really is a quick mix-it-up-in-one-bowl and slap-it-on (literally) job. You can use a food processor to chop the prawns, just add a couple of ice cubes to keep them cool, and use the pause function! This is the Chinese way to use up left over bread, and it's perfect as a canapé, starter, snack or a side dish.

METHOD

1. **Prep:** Combine all the ingredients for the prawn paste in a bowl. Cook a teaspoon of the filling to check and adjust the seasoning before assembling the whole batch.

2. Trim off the bread crust and cut into quarters. Heap a teaspoon of the prawn paste onto each square, use a dinner knife to spread the paste over the square of bread. Make sure to spread to the edges. Sprinkle with sesame seeds.

3. **Cook:** Fill a wok or deep saucepan half full with oil, heat on a medium high heat. Place the handle of a wooden spoon into the oil, when bubbles gather around the handle promptly, the oil is hot enough for frying. Alternatively, use a food thermometer and heat to 180°C.

4. Use a slotted spoon to lower the prawn toast into the oil to avoid splashing. Fry only a handful at a time, overcrowding would lower the oil temperature and the bread will get greasy.

5. Turn occasionally to ensure even browning, transfer to some paper towels to drain when it is golden brown, about 6 - 7 minutes.

6. **Serve:** With your favourite chilli sauce.

CHEF'S TIPS

1. If the bread is fresh and fluffy, spread the slices out on a tray to 'dry out' as it is easier to spread the prawn paste onto firmer bread.
2. In the photograph opposite, I used mini sour dough baguette slices instead of sandwich slices.

中国 CHINA

BEEF IN BLACK BEAN SAUCE

Serves: 2

Prep time: 15 minutes

Cook time: 15 minutes

INGREDIENTS

Beef Marinade

300g sirloin or
rump steak

1 tsp cornflour

1 tsp light soy sauce

½ tsp ground white
pepper

Stir fry ingredients

2 tbsp vegetable oil

1 onion, sliced

1 red bell pepper,
deseeded and sliced

2 tbsp black bean garlic
sauce

4 spring onions, 3cm
lengths

1 tsp toasted sesame oil

Serving suggestions

Fluffy rice (page 44)

Garlic pak choy (page 82)

A classic Cantonese dish that can be found on every menu in Chinese restaurants and takeaways across the globe. Black bean sauce is made from salt-preserved fermented soyabeans. Whole beans are used when you want a savoury pop, but if you want the flavour to be distributed throughout the dish, the shop-bought black bean and garlic sauce in jars works beautifully.
It is convenient, stores well, and has a depth of savoury flavour.

METHOD

1. **Marinate:** Remove any sinew and tendon from the steak. Cutting against the grain, slice the beef into strips. Mix with the beef marinade ingredients, set aside.

2. **Cook:** Heat a wok or frying pan over a high heat until smoking. Drizzle 1 tbsp of the oil over the pan and heat again. Sear the beef until it is brown on all sides but not fully cooked. Fry in batches if your pan is small, or if the heat is weak. The meat should caramelise and not boil. Rest on a plate.

3. Drizzle the rest of the oil over the pan, fry the onions for 1 minutes until they are fragrant. Add the peppers and fry until soft but still firm, for about 1 - 2 minutes. Stir in the sauce, spring onions, beef and sesame oil, toss briefly.

4. **Serve:** With rice, and perhaps a stir-fried green such as pak choy.

CHEF'S TIPS

1. Use an authentic brand of black bean sauce. My personal preference is Lee Kum Kee. Some brands are more salty or stronger in flavour than others, taste and adjust to your personal preference.
2. Adding the sesame oil at the last minute retains the fragrance and nutty flavour of this delicate oil.

GARLIC PAK CHOY

Serves: 2-3

Prep time: 5 minutes

Cook time: 5 minutes

INGREDIENTS

1 tbsp vegetable oil

2 garlic cloves,
chopped chunky

250g pak choy

Sauce

1 tsp cornflour

2 tbsp oyster sauce

2 tbsp Chinese
Shaoxing wine, or if
unavailable, dry sherry

2 tbsp water

Serving suggestions

Fluffy rice (page 44)

Beef in black bean sauce
(page 80)

I prefer to eat my pak choy crisp and crunchy. So they get tossed in a fiery wok for a mere count of ten, the sauces are added, then a quick thickening of the liquid with a little cornflour mixed with water. The thickened sauce coats and clings to each piece of the pak choy, giving it uniform flavour and a lovely feel in the mouth.

METHOD

1. **Prep:** Trim and discard the base of the pak choy, separate each stem from the core, wash thoroughly and drain well. Split each stem into half lengthwise and place on your cooking clock (see chef's tips).

2. Add all the sauce ingredients in a bowl, mix and set aside.

3. **Cook:** Heat a wok or frying pan over a high heat. Add the oil followed by the chopped garlic, stirring constantly until lightly golden. Be careful not to burn the garlic as it will taste bitter.

4. Add the pak choy, stir 10 times. Add the sauce and stir until it thickens.

5. **Serve:** With rice, noodles, or other Chinese dishes.

CHEF'S TIPS

Cooking clock - a brilliant concept to organise your ingredients and cooking sequence. Lay out the ingredients on a plate or tray, the ingredient that is cooked first will be positioned at 12 o'clock, the rest of the ingredients follow according to the length of time they will take to cook. For example, any root vegetables will be positioned at an earlier time (say 3 o'clock) than green leafy vegetables (say 6 o'clock), and any herbs or garnishes will be placed in the last position at 11 o'clock. Try it out for any cuisine, it is especially useful for quick stir frying as time is of the essence in the presence of a hot wok.

GOLDEN EGG FRIED RICE

Serves: 2

Prep time: Overnight rice + 5 minutes

Cook time: 10 minutes

INGREDIENTS

300g cooked cooled overnight rice, (fluffy rice page 44)

3 eggs, separate yolk and white

1 tsp sea salt

½ tsp ground white pepper

2 tbsp vegetable oil

2 garlic cloves, roughly chopped

2 spring onions, finely sliced

Golden fried rice got its name because of its beautiful golden hue. It is achieved by coating the rice completely in egg yolk before you stir-fry. I find that most organic eggs have deep golden yolks, but you can also add a pinch of ground turmeric to guarantee colour. I have kept the ingredients simple to showcase the rich and fragrant egg aroma.

The secret to a good fried rice? Heat control! You will be rewarded with what the Chinese call 'wok's breath', the lovely smoky flavour and aroma of stir-fried dishes from restaurant kitchens and street vendors. Heat your pan to smoking point before you add oil (which should have a high smoke point, such as vegetable oil), then heat the oil until it is hot and swirl it round the pan. This will also help prevent food from sticking to the pan. A non-stick pan is not suitable because the non-stick coating does not tolerate high heat. Domestic hobs don't normally give out enough heat, so the trick is to keep portions small and cook in batches. It is easy to achieve once you learn the tips and technique.

METHOD

1. Coat the chilled cooked rice with the egg yolk. Season with salt and pepper then set aside.

2. Heat the wok over a high heat until smoking. Add 1 tbsp of oil, heat it again and swirl it around the wok, fry the garlic for 30 seconds, until lightly golden.

    Be careful not to burn it. Stir in the rice and fry over a very high heat for 2 minutes. Push the rice aside, add 1 tbsp of oil then scramble the egg white before mixing with the rice.

3. Add the spring onions, stir to combine and transfer to a serving dish.

CHEF'S TIPS

1. The secret to a good 'bouncy' fried rice is to use left over rice; rice that has been cooked, promptly chilled and left overnight in the fridge.
2. Make sure that the fried rice is piping hot before serving.

KUNG PAO PRAWNS

Serves: 2

Prep time: 10 minutes

Cook time: 5 minutes

INGREDIENTS

Prawn marinade

300g raw prawns, shelled and deveined

1 tsp ground white pepper

1 teaspoon cornflour

Sauce

1 tsp cornflour

1 tsp light soy sauce

1 tsp dark soy sauce

1 tsp Worcestershire sauce

1 tsp sesame oil

1 tbsp Chinese black vinegar/balsamic vinegar

1 tbsp runny honey

1 tbsp Shaoxing rice wine/dry sherry

4 tbsp water

Stir-fry

2 tbsp vegetable oil

15 dried chillies, cut in half and deseeded

4 garlic cloves, sliced

3cm cube fresh ginger, sliced

4 spring onions, cut on the slant 2cm lengths

2 tbsp roasted salted peanuts

1 tsp sesame oil

1 tsp Sichuan peppercorn, ground

Kung pao, Gong bao or Kung po - different names for the same stir-fried dish. The original Sichuan version uses chicken but prawns are a popular alternative. Dried chillies are an iconic ingredient in Kung Pao dishes, it provides flavour and a little spice, but they are not meant to be eaten, just suck the sauce off them and discard.

METHOD

1. **Prep:** Combine all the 'prawn marinade' ingredients in a bowl. Mix all the sauce ingredients in a separate bowl. Set aside.

2. **Cook:** Heat a wok on a high heat until smoking, drizzle 1 tbsp of the oil around the wok. Stir in the prawns and fry until they start to turn pink. Remove to a plate and set aside, do not overcook the prawns to prevent them from getting rubbery.

3. Lower to a medium heat, add the rest of the oil and fry the chilli, garlic and ginger for 1 minute until they are fragrant. Return the prawns to the wok, add the spring onions, peanuts, ground Szechuan peppercorn and sauce. Stir until the sauce is thicken.

4. **Serve**.

CHEF'S TIPS

You can swap peanuts for cashew nuts.

印度 INDIA

GREEN CHUTNEY

Serves: 4

Prep time: 10 minutes + 10 minutes soaking times

This tangy, spicy and aromatic side dish is eaten with all kinds of Indian snacks, chaat, wraps etc. Apart from adding zing to your palette it provides great health benefits too. Fresh coriander and mint are super-herbs, aiding digestion and helping to detoxify the body.

INGREDIENTS

50g fresh coriander

25g fresh mint

2cm length ginger

2 garlic cloves

2 green chillies

1 tsp ground cumin

1 tsp sea salt

1 tsp caster sugar

2 tbsp cider/wine vinegar

4 tbsp water

METHOD

1. Pick off the mint leaves and discard the stalk. Coriander stalks have a lot of flavour so keep them attached. Soak the mint leaves with the coriander in a bowl for 10 minutes to plump them up.

2. Peel the ginger by scraping with a teaspoon. Remove the seeds from the chillies for a less spicy chutney, cut into chunks.

3. Blend all the ingredients together until you get a smooth consistency. Adjust the seasoning, store in an airtight container in the fridge. It'll keep fresh for about 3 days, freeze any extra on the day it is made.

CHEF'S TIPS

1. A handheld blender produces a finer and smoother consistency.
2. If you are using a food processor, add a couple of ice cubes to keep the mixture cooler and the colour vibrant and green.

GARLIC CORIANDER YOGHURT DIP

Serves: 2

Prep time: 5 minutes

This is a very versatile dip, use it as a marinade to give flavour and to tenderise. Brilliant with grilled meats and seafood as a sauce, and you can also use it to dress salads.

INGREDIENTS

4 tbsp Greek yoghurt, full fat

1 tbsp fresh coriander leaves and stem, chopped

1 clove garlic, crushed

½ tsp sea salt

METHOD

1. Combine all the ingredients and mix well.

CHEF'S TIPS

It will keep fresh in an air-tight container for 3 - 4 days, in the fridge.

NO FUSS FLATBREAD

Makes: 4 flatbreads

Prep time: 15 minutes

Cook time: 20 minutes

INGREDIENTS

200g self-raising flour, plus extra for dusting

200ml plain yoghurt, full fat

1 tsp cumin seeds

½ tsp salt

1 tbsp salted butter, melted

4 sprigs fresh coriander, chopped

I promise you that this is really what it says ... no fuss! Knocked out in such a short time, you will wonder why you have never attempted to make flatbread before.

METHOD

1. Mix the flour, cumin seeds and salt in a bowl, then add the yoghurt and stir with a wooden spoon to make a soft dough. Cover the bowl with a damp cloth and set aside for 10 minutes.

2. Dust the work surface with some flour. Tip the dough onto the floured surface, dust your hands with flour and knead for 1 minute until the dough is smooth. Divide the dough into 4 pieces, roll out to about 3mm thick.

3. In a dry non-stick frying pan, cook the flatbread on a medium high heat for about 2 minutes on each side until specks of brown appear, and the dough slightly rises. Keep warm on a plate covered with a clean damp tea towel.

4. Wipe the frying pan in between cooking each flatbread to remove traces of flour.

5. Brush with the melted butter and sprinkle with coriander to serve.

CHEF'S TIPS

1. Best eaten fresh.
2. Sweet fennel seeds are a delightful alternative to cumin seeds.
3. Fresh mint is a good substitute if you do not have coriander.

SPICED LAMB SKEWERS

Makes: 8 skewers

Prep time: 10 minutes

Cook time: 15 minutes

INGREDIENTS

500g minced lamb

2 tbsp tikka curry powder (see chef's tips)

1 medium onion

2 garlic cloves

2 tbsp fresh coriander leaves and stalk

1 tbsp fresh mint – leaves only

½ to 1 tsp sea salt (check for salt content in the curry powder, adjust to taste)

To cook

8 bamboo or metal skewers

1 tsp vegetable oil mixed with 1 tbsp of water, for basting

Serving suggestions

Flatbread (page 92)

Garlic coriander yoghurt dip (page 91)

Green chutney (page 90)

These skewers are perfectly balanced with aromatic spices and fresh herbs. Whether grilled on a barbecue or pan-fried, they bring a taste of Middle Eastern and Asian street food right to your home. Another easy recipe to add to your repertoire.

METHOD

1. If you are using bamboo skewers, fully immerse them in a dish of cold tap water for 10 minutes to prevent the skewers from catching fire on the grill.

2. Finely chop the onion, garlic and herbs, add to a large mixing bowl with the other ingredients and mix thoroughly with your hands. Divide into 8 portions, mould firmly around the skewers in a long sausage shape.

3. Brush lightly with the oil and water mixture, and grill on a medium heat until brown on all sides and cooked through, allow 2 - 3 minutes.

CHEF'S TIPS

1. Use a more spicy curry powder if desired.
2. Make mini versions to serve as canapés for a drinks party, mould the meat mixture around short skewers or lollipop sticks.

TANDOORI SALMON TACOS

Serves: 4

Prep time: 5 minutes

Cook time: 10 minutes

INGREDIENTS

500g fresh salmon
(4 fillets), cubed

4 tsp Greek yoghurt,
full fat

3 tsp tandoori spice mix
½ to 1 tsp sea salt
(see chef's tips)

2 tsp vegetable oil

4 folded flatbread,
or pitta bread

Serving suggestions

Garlic Coriander
yoghurt dip (page 91)

No fuss flatbread
(page 92)

The quickest and easiest week day meal, three main ingredients - salmon, yoghurt and tandoori spice. This recipe can also be tweaked for a dinner party.

METHOD

1. Marinate the salmon in the yoghurt, spice and salt for 2 minutes.

2. You can either pan-fry or grill the salmon.

3. **To pan-fry:** Heat the frying pan on a medium high heat. Add the oil then the salmon, space them slightly apart and caramelise on all sides (2-3 minutes). If the pan is overcrowded, the salmon will release moisture and they will boil instead of fry.

4. **Or grill:** Thread the salmon onto metal skewers, brush with the oil and cook on a barbecue or under an overhead grill.

5. Wet your hands with cold tap water, pat the bread to moisten them. Refresh them in a frying pan or toaster for a minute until they are warmed through. Keep warm on a plate under a clean and slightly dampened teacloth.

6. Fill the breads with the salmon and a dollop of yoghurt dip.

CHEF'S TIPS
1. Check for salt content in the tandoori spice mix, adjust accordingly before adding salt.
2. Using the same recipe, replace the salmon with raw king prawns, tofu or chicken to create a new dish. Marinate the prawns or tofu for the same amount of time as the salmon. Cut slits in the chicken with a knife, and marinate them for at least half an hour, or overnight if you can, to allow the seasoning to penetrate.

KOREA

BEEF BULGOGI

Serves: 2

Prep time: 5 minutes

Marinate: 10 minutes

Cook time: 5 minutes

INGREDIENTS

450g beef, sirloin/
ribeye/rump steaks

2 tbsp vegetable oil

Marinade

4 large garlic cloves

1 large onion

1 pear, peel and core

2cm cube fresh ginger,
peel

1 spring onion,
finely sliced

1 tbsp light brown sugar

1 tbsp sesame oil

3 tbsp light soy sauce

½ tsp ground
black pepper

1 tsp white sesame seeds

Serve

Sliced spring onion
and lettuce

Fluffy rice (page 44)

'Bul' means fire in Korean, and 'gogi' is a general term for meat. Beef is most commonly used for bulgogi, chicken and pork are less popular. It is typically cooked over an open flame but can also be cooked in a frying pan at home. Korean pears are added to tenderize the meat and for flavour; you can use any firm pears instead. For cheaper/tougher cuts of meat, add a teaspoon of grated pineapple or kiwi to the existing marinade. They are strong tenderizing agents so keep to the recommended quantity and time.

METHOD

1. **Prep:** Slice the beef as thin as possible, about 3mm thick (see chef's tips).

2. Cut the garlic, onion, pear and ginger into chunks, blitz in a food processor until smooth. Pour into a large bowl. Add the rest of the marinade ingredients and the sliced beef and mix well. Cover and leave in the fridge for 10 minutes.

3. **Cook:** Heat up a griddle pan over a high heat until it starts smoking. Brush some vegetable oil onto the pan then add the beef slices leaving little gaps between them. Cook in batches, do not overcrowd the pan, otherwise the beef will create steam and the meat will start to boil instead of caramelising. The beef will cook quickly as it is so thin. (2 minutes)

4. **Serve:** Garnish with spring onions and sesame seeds. Eat the beef wrapped in a lettuce leaf, accompanied with rice.

CHEF'S TIPS

It is easier to cut beef into very thin slices after it is partially frozen. Trim off any tendons and sinews first, then place the beef in the freezer for an hour before slicing to the desired thickness.

JAPCHAE (SWEET POTATO NOODLES)

Serves: 4

Prep time: 20 minutes

Cook time: 10 minutes

INGREDIENTS

Sauce

1 tbsp toasted white sesame seeds

2 tbsp light brown sugar

2 tbsp sesame oil

4 tbsp light soy sauce

1 tsp cracked black pepper

2 tsp minced garlic

Stir fry ingredients

300g sirloin/ ribeye steak

½ tsp sea salt

1 onion, sliced

1 carrot, fine strips

1 red capsicum pepper, sliced.

5 shitake mushrooms, sliced

100g spinach

200g sweet potato noodles (see chef's tips)

2 tbsp vegetable oil

These noodles are chewy and light in texture, with colourful vegetables dressed in sesame, soy and garlic. This is a stir fry dish that can be eaten hot or at room temperature. Instead of cooking every single ingredient separately, I have simplified the process for the same delicious treat.

METHOD

1. **Prep:** Trim off the fat and sinew from the steak, slice thinly cutting against the grain. Marinate with the salt and set aside. Slice all the vegetables, set aside in separate clusters on a plate. Combine all the sauce ingredients in a very large mixing bowl, mix to dissolve the sugar and set aside.

2. **Cook:** Bring a large saucepan of water to a boil, blanch the spinach for 30 seconds. Transfer to a bowl of cold water with a perforated spoon, drain and squeeze the water from the spinach, place in the mixing bowl.

3. Re-boil the water, cook the noodles for 4-5 minutes until translucent and cooked through. Drain in a colander, rinse under a cold tap.

Snip the noodles with a pair of scissors into 10cm lengths, add to the bowl.

4. Heat up 1 tbsp of the oil in a large frying pan until smoking, sear the beef and add to the bowl. Drizzle another tbsp of oil around the pan. Fry the onions for 30 seconds, add the carrots and cook for 1 minute, add the mushrooms to cook for 1 minute then the peppers for another minute. Add them all to the bowl. Add the carrots and cook for 1 minute, then add the mushrooms (another minute), followed by the pepper (1 minute). Add them all to the bowl.

5. **Serve:** Toss well to combine and serve at room temperature. If you prefer the noodles hot, return them to the frying pan to warm through.

CHEF'S TIPS

1. Instead of the Korean sweet potato noodles, you can use glass noodles instead, they're not as thick or chewy but have a similar smooth texture. Glass noodles are also known as mung bean vermicelli or cellophane noodles.
2. Left-over noodles from the fridge will look opaque and taste hard. Reheat them in a frying pan or microwave oven, and it will be soft and chewy again.

KOREAN FRIED CHICKEN (KFC)

Serves: 6

Prep time: 10 minutes

Cook time: 25 minutes

INGREDIENTS

Chicken

1 kg chicken wings, or boneless chicken thighs cut in half

½ tsp sea salt

½ tsp ground white pepper

2 tbsp mirin rice wine

8 tbsp cornflour

6 tbsp self-raising flour

1 litre vegetable oil for deep frying

Glaze

3 cloves fresh garlic, chopped

1 tbsp light soy sauce

2 tbsp rice/cider vinegar

5 tbsp runny honey

5 tbsp tomato ketchup

3 tbsp gochujang, Korean fermented red pepper paste

Garnish

1 tsp toasted sesame seeds

The locals often pan fried chicken with beer as a snack or an easy dinner solution. The glaze is a little spicy but hugely additive, serve it on the side for a non-spicy option.

METHOD

1. **Prep Chicken:** Marinate the chicken in salt, pepper and mirin for 10 minutes. Mix the cornflour and self-raising flour, set aside to coat the marinated chicken pieces after the 10 minutes.

2. **Make the glaze:** Simmer all the glaze ingredients in a pan for 1 minute.

3. **Deep frying:** Fill a wok or deep saucepan 1/3 full with oil, heat to 180°C. To check, place the handle of a wooden spoon into the oil. When bubbles gather around the handle the oil is hot enough. Fry the chicken in batches for 3 minutes until lightly golden. Rest the fried chicken for 15 minutes.

4. Reheat the oil, and re-fry the chicken pieces a second time over a high heat until golden brown, about 2 minutes. Fry in batches. Place on a wire rack to drain off the excess oil.

5. **Serve:** Brush the glaze over the chicken with a pastry brush, garnish with sesame seeds.

CHEF'S TIPS

The secret is in the double frying technique - the first fry releases the fat from the chicken skin, the resting allows the chicken to retain its moisture and the second fry locks in the crispness. It stays crispy for a couple of hours.

SPICY CUCUMBER SALAD

Serves: 6 side portions

Prep time: 10 minutes

INGREDIENTS

1 large cucumber

½ tsp sea salt

Dressing

1 tbsp toasted sesame oil

1 tbsp gochujang, Korean fermented red pepper paste

1 tbsp rice or cider vinegar

½ tbsp light soy sauce

½ tbsp runny honey

Serve

1 tbsp toasted white sesame seeds

Light and refreshing, this salad leaves your mouth tingling from the punchy spiced dressing! The method used to smash the whole cucumber is a classic Chinese technique to crack the skin and split the flesh into appealing craggy pieces releasing the seeds and to get the dressing absorbed right into the cucumber. It is really quick and easy. Omit the chilli paste if you prefer a non-spicy version but I would recommend you try it at least once.

METHOD

1. Cut off the tips of the cucumber at both ends, smash the whole cucumber with the side of a large knife (or you could use a rolling pin) until it splits into quarters and look jagged. Cut into irregular bitesize pieces removing all the seeds.

2. Add the salt, mix well and leave in a colander to drain for 10 minutes.

3. In the meantime, combine the ingredients for the dressing in a large bowl, set aside.

4. Pat the cucumber pieces dry with paper towels, add to the dressing and toss lightly. Sprinkle with sesame seeds and serve.

CHEF'S TIPS

1. Salting and draining the cucumber will draw out moisture, giving it more crunch and flavour
2. To prevent the dressing getting watered down, toss the cucumber in the dressing at the last minute before serving.

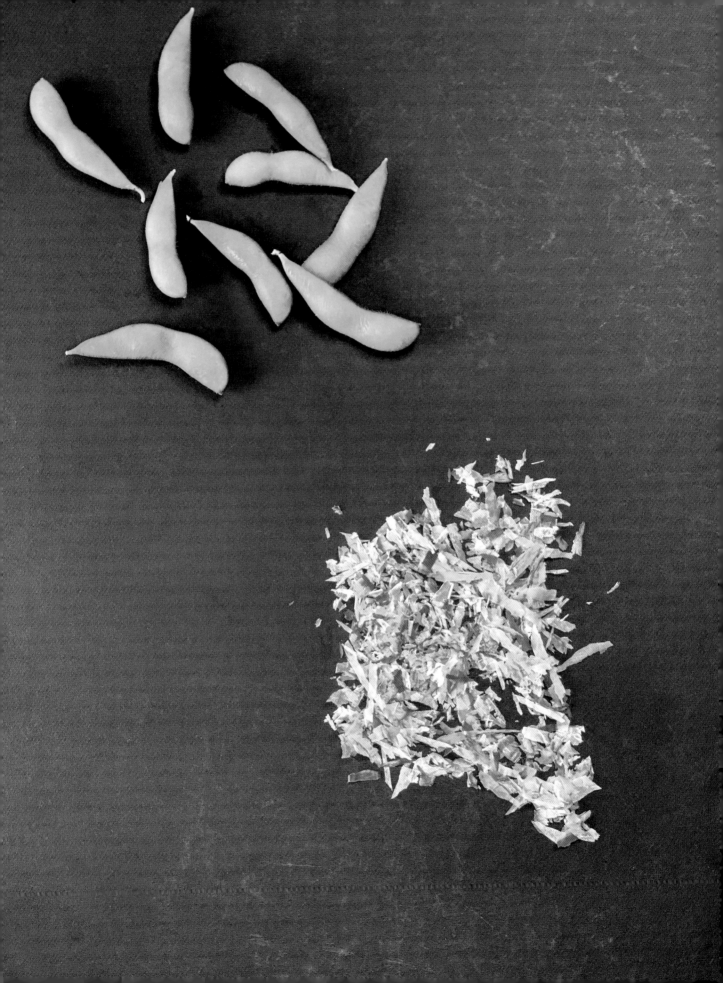

日本 JAPAN

BEEF GYOZA

Makes: 32 to 35

Prep time: 20 minutes

Cook time: 10 minutes

INGREDIENTS

1 packet gyoza wrappers, defrosted (32 to 35 depending on brand)

4 tbsp vegetable oil for pan frying

Filling

400g minced beef, 12% fat

200g white cabbage, 1cm cubes

½ tsp sea salt

½ tsp castor sugar

½ tsp ground white pepper

2 tsp toasted sesame oil

2 tsp light soy sauce

1 tsp fresh ginger, grated

Serve

Citrus ponzu dip (page 112)

A Japanese dumpling inspired by the Chinese "Jiaozi" dumpling. Thin pastry filled with meat and vegetables, usually pork or chicken with cabbage. You can create your own versions to your heart's content - you can combine tofu with edamame beans for a vegan version, and why not make minced turkey, spring onions and shitake mushroom gyoza at Christmas?

METHOD

1. **Filling:** Combine all the ingredients for the filling in a bowl. Cook a teaspoon of the filling to check and adjust the seasoning before assembling the whole batch.

2. **Make gyoza:** Place a teaspoon of filling onto the middle of a wrapper, moisten the edge with water. Fold the wrapper over to form a half moon sealing the contents without air pockets inside. Make 4 pleats along the edge of the dumpling. Repeat using up all the wrappers. (Make meatballs with any extra fillings).

3. **Cook:** Heat the oil in a frying pan on a medium heat. Swirl it around the pan then place in a few dumplings, spaced slightly apart. Shallow-fry the dumplings until the bottoms are lightly golden, around 1 minute. Add 2 tablespoons of cold tap water to the pan, cover with a tight-fitting lid. Steam the dumplings for 2 minutes, remove the lid and allow the base of the dumplings to crisp up again. Test they are cooked by piercing with a sharp knife. Clear juices oozing out indicate they are ready.

CHEF'S TIPS

1. Cook a teaspoon of filling to taste, adjust the seasoning if needed before assembling the whole batch.
2. Freeze the gyoza uncooked. Cook these 'dumplings on demand' from frozen whenever you fancy some. Increase the cooking time slightly and ensure that it is piping hot before serving.

CITRUS PONZU DIP

Makes: Roughly 150ml

Prep time: 5 minutes

INGREDIENTS

1 tsp castor sugar/runny honey/agave syrup

1 tsp fresh ginger, finely grated (see chef's tips)

1 tbsp rice/cider vinegar

2 tbsp water

2 tbsp fresh lemon juice with zest (roughly 1 lemon)

2 tbsp mirin rice wine

4 tbsp light soy sauce

Ponzu sauce is a classic Japanese dipping sauce, tangy and umami rich. Wonderfully versatile, it is great used as a dipping sauce for cold noodles, for dressing salads, with grilled meat or fish, and used in a stir-fry. It is also delicious with gyoza, sushi and sashimi. The word ponzu is made up of 'pon' and 'su', where 'pon' means 'punch' and 'su' means vinegar. Traditionally this sauce has a 'sea flavour' undertone, you can add kombu, bonito flakes or even nori to recreate that flavour if you wish. Simply infuse with the rest of the ingredients in this recipe.

METHOD

1. Combine all the ingredients and stir until the sugar is dissolved. It is ready to be served.

2. If you prefer a clear dipping sauce, allow the ingredients to seep for 2 minutes then strain.

CHEF'S TIPS

1. Frozen ginger is easier to grate, has a smoother texture and is less fibrous. To freeze ginger, peel and cut the fresh ginger into thumbnail size pieces and seal in a freezer bag or container. Remove the quantity you need and grate from frozen

2. This sauce will keep for a couple of weeks in an airtight container. Use a dry clean spoon each time you scoop out some sauce.

SMOKED SALMON NIGIRI BALLS

Makes: 16

Prep time: 20 minutes

Cook time: 12 minutes

INGREDIENTS

200ml sushi rice, uncooked

280ml water

200g smoked salmon

Sushi vinegar

15ml rice vinegar

½ tsp sea salt

2 tsp castor sugar

Serve

Light soy sauce

Wasabi

This is such an easy way to make sushi at home without any special equipment. Sushi does not have to be made with raw fish, smoked salmon is more widely available, cheaper, and has a longer shelf life than raw salmon. These little balls are so pretty, fun to make and taste so good.

METHOD

1. **Sushi vinegar:** Dissolve the salt and sugar in the rice vinegar.

2. **Cook rice:** Wash the rice by gently swishing it in the saucepan with your fingers, the water will turn a milky white colour. Drain, add fresh water and swish the rice again. Repeat this 3 to 4 times until the water runs clear. Drain in a sieve and return the rice to the saucepan.

3. Add the 280ml of water, and bring to a boil over a medium heat. Stir then cover with the lid and reduce to the lowest heat setting. Check after 10 minutes, if all the water is absorbed, remove from the heat. Rest the rice for 2 minutes.

4. **Cool rice:** Put the rice on a tray. Pour over the sushi vinegar. Using a diagonal cutting and turning motion, GENTLY turn the rice with a flat wooden spoon to incorporate the sushi vinegar and to cool the rice. You can use a paper or electric fan to speed up the cooling process. The grains should feel firm and look shiny. Be careful not to handle the rice too much as it may become mushy. Divide the rice into 16 portions, set aside.

5. **Assembling:** Cut the smoked salmon slices into 16 pieces. Place one piece on a square of cling film and place a portion of rice on top. Bring the 4 corners of the cling film together to meet in the middle and twist to form a tight little ball. Present the nigiri balls with the salmon on top of the rice.

6. **Serve:** With soy sauce and wasabi.

CHEF'S TIPS

Sushi is best when eaten on the day it is made. Although it can be kept in the fridge for a day or two, the rice will become chalky. Do not make pieces of sushi to be eaten the next day. Store any excess rice in a covered container in the fridge. Reheat it the next day and the rice will be soft and fluffy again; cool the rice and you can then make your sushi.

TERIYAKI SALMON

Serves: 2

Prep time: 10 minutes

Cook time: 10 minutes

INGREDIENTS

2 pcs salmon fillets
(roughly 150g each)

1 tbsp plain flour

1 tbsp vegetable oil

**Teriyaki glaze
(see chef's tips)**

2 tsp brown sugar

1 tbsp light soy sauce

2 tbsp mirin

2 tbsp water

½ tsp fresh ginger,
grated

½ tsp fresh garlic,
grated

Serving suggestions

Garnish with toasted
white sesame seeds and
sliced spring onions

Fluffy rice (page 44)

Garlic pak choy
(page 82)

Edamame beans

"Teri" means "lustre or gleam" and "yaki" means to grill or cook over direct heat. Traditionally made with 4 ingredients – soy, mirin, sake and sugar - it is thickened by simmering and reduction. It's so easy to make and so versatile. Use it as a marinade for meat, seafood, vegetables and tofu; as a glaze brushed over your grilled or pan-fried dishes for that deliciously sticky savoury flavour; or as a sauce in stir-fries. For this recipe, we have removed the sake and added a hint of ginger and garlic to complement the salmon.

METHOD

1. Combine the ingredients for the sauce in a bowl.

2. Dust the salmon with the flour.

3. Heat a frying pan over a medium heat, add the oil. Place the salmon, skin side down, in the pan and fry for 2 - 3 minutes until the skin is crispy. Flip over and fry for 30 seconds. Pour the sauce around the salmon, to keep the skin crispy, simmer for 2 minute.

4. Garnish with sesame seeds and spring onion and serve.

5. **Serve:** With rice, boiled edamame beans or Chinese greens.

CHEF'S TIPS

1. If you prefer a sauce to a glaze, add 2 tablespoons of water mixed with 1 teaspoon of cornflour towards the end of the cooking.
2. Adjust the cooking time according to the thickness of the fillet and how pink you would like your salmon.

TREATS

LEMONGRASS MOJITO

Serves: 1

Prep time: 10 minutes

INGREDIENTS

50ml dark rum

1 lemongrass stalk

2 tbsp light brown sugar

1 lime, cut into wedges

4 mint leaves, plus
2 sprigs for garnish

Ice

Ginger ale, chilled

Equipment

Measuring jigger

Muddler or small rolling
pin with a flat end

Tall tumbler glass

Mojitos are traditionally made with white rum, cane sugar, lime, mint and a splash of soda. At Lilian's Kitchen, our motto is to 'Bring a Taste of Asia to You' so I keep true to my word by using ingredients popular in Asia to transform the taste and also to add some health benefits.

Lemongrass is added to this fusion cocktail because it is widely grown in Asia and known for its antioxidant and anti-inflammatory benefits. Instead of soda, ginger ale is used, as ginger has been used for centuries to aid digestion, reduce nausea, and help fight the flu and common cold. Dark rum is used instead of white rum, as it is matured in oak barrels and has a deeper, richer and more complex flavour and overtones. Brown sugar is used instead of cane sugar for its lovely caramel and vanilla flavours. The citrus kick of lime and refreshing fragrance of mint remain. You should definitely try this concoction - it is truly a delicious combination!

METHOD

1. Remove the tough outer layer from the lemongrass. Cut off 2cm of the bulbous part of the lemongrass and chop very finely. Reserve the stalk.

2. Drop the chopped lemongrass and sugar into a tall glass, mush with the muddler or rolling pin.

3. Add the lime wedges, mint leaves and rum, mush gently to release all the flavours.

4. Fill the glass with ice and top up with the chilled ginger ale.

5. Garnish with the lemongrass stalk and a sprig of fresh mint.

MANGO LASSI

Serves: 2 - 3

Prep time: 10 minutes

INGREDIENTS

250g mango puree, fresh or frozen

250ml plain yoghurt, full fat

120ml water or milk, chilled

2 tbsp caster sugar or runny honey

2 pcs green cardamom pods

Originating from ancient India, lassi is a blended drink of yoghurt, water and spices. You can enjoy a sweet or salty lassi, adding fruits and sugar to sweeten or salt for the savoury.

Temperatures in India can climb to 42°C (108°F) in summer and very few people have air conditioning, so it is hot and sweaty everywhere you go. People try to keep cool by wearing light cotton clothing, maximising shade and drinking cold beverages. Locals still look forward to their summer despite the heat because as they have amazing mangoes to savour in the summer season.

The blended combination of sweet ripe mango, yoghurt and ice with a sprinkling of crushed cardamom will truly hit a sweet spot. Sounds fabulous, doesn't it? Whisk up a batch of this mango lassi at home now!

METHOD

1. Remove the seeds from the cardamom pods and crush finely. Set aside.

2. Blitz all the remaining ingredients in an electric jug or hand blender until smooth.

3. Serve in a tall glass with a sprinkling of crushed cardamom.

CHEF'S TIPS

Even more delicious left to infuse in the fridge for an hour. Serve chilled from the fridge.

MANGO STICKY RICE

Serves: 4

Prep time: 20 minutes

Cook time: 30 minutes

INGREDIENTS

200g glutinous rice

2 ripe mangoes

250ml coconut milk, Chaokoh or Aroy-D brand

½ tsp sea salt

100g caster sugar

2 tsp cornflour

Sticky rice is also known as glutinous rice or sweet rice. It is a short grain rice and it earned this name because it sticks together readily when cooked. The term glutinous refers to its glue-like or sticky texture but it does not contain gluten. It is also not sweet despite being called sweet rice. So, sweet rice, glutinous rice and sticky rice all refer to the same type of rice, characterised by its sticky texture. It is used in both sweet or savoury dishes and available from major supermarkets or online by searching 'glutinous rice'.

METHOD

1. **Rice:** Soak the glutinous rice in cold tap water for 10 minutes.

2. Line a steamer with a wet muslin cloth. Drain the rice, then spread it evenly on the cloth and fold the corners of the cloth over the rice. Cover the steamer and ensure a tight fit over the pan. Steam the rice over boiling water for 15 minutes. Don't worry if it looks more dry than normal cooked rice. The rice is cooked when it doesn't taste chalky. If necessary, steam for another 5 minutes. Check that there is sufficient water in the pan for further steaming.

3. **Prep mango:** While the rice is cooking, skin, deseed and cut the mangoes into slices or cubes, cover and set aside.

4. **Sauce:** Heat up the coconut milk, sugar and salt on a low heat, stirring until the grains have dissolved. Do not boil. Reserve 100ml to add to the cooked glutinous rice. Thicken the remaining coconut milk with the cornflour mixed with 2 teaspoons of cold tap water.

5. When the rice is cooked, transfer it into a large bowl and gently stir in the 100ml unthicken coconut milk, without breaking up the rice. Cover the bowl and leave the rice for 5 minutes to absorb the coconut milk.

6. **Serve:** At room temperature with the mangoes and thickened coconut milk.

CHEF'S TIPS

1. My favourite brands of coconut milk are Chaokoh and Aroy-D, both widely available. They have a rich and pleasing coconut taste, and a high proportion of coconut fat.
2. You can also cook the rice in a rice cooker or on the hob.

MISO TOFFEE PINEAPPLE

Serves: 4

Prep time: 10 minutes

Cook time: 20 minutes

INGREDIENTS

1 medium ripe pineapple

1 tsp oil, neutral flavour like rapeseed or canola, mix with 1 tsp water

Toffee sauce

150g light brown sugar

75g salted butter

120ml double cream

2 tsp white miso paste

Serve (optional)

Vanilla ice cream

This tropical fruit evokes memories of sunshine and happiness, and something magical happens when you cook pineapple: it becomes sweeter and juicier! Quick and easy, this grilled pineapple recipe is not just for your summer barbecues, you can cook it on a griddle pan indoors. I love the grill marks on them, it is visually appealing and the direct contact with the grill caramelises the fruit and produces new and wonderful flavours. The miso adds an extra depth of flavour to the toffee sauce, making it even more delicious!

METHOD

1. **Toffee sauce:** Place the sugar, butter and cream in a saucepan. Bring to a gentle boil stirring regularly for 2 minutes. Add the miso paste, stir and set aside.

2. **Pineapple:** Cut off the top and bottom of the pineapple. Stand the pineapple upright and slice off the skin in strips from top to bottom, following the curve of the fruit. Cut just deep enough to remove the 'eyes' of the pineapple. Split into quarters lengthwise, cut off the core from each quarter, and slice each quarter in half lengthwise again, so you have 8 long pieces.

3. **Cook:** Lightly brush with the oil and water mixture. Grill on a griddle pan or barbecue over a medium high heat for 2 minutes on each side. Leave the pineapple to caramelise and get good contact with the grate for beautiful grill marks.

4. **Serve:** With miso toffee sauce and perhaps a dollop of vanilla ice cream.

CHEF'S TIPS

Cutting the pineapple lengthwise ensures each portion has a fair distribution of flavour, as the bottom half of a pineapple is sweeter than the top half.

SEXY WOBBLE PANNA COTTA

Serves: 6

Prep time: 5 minutes

Cook time: 10 minutes

Plus chilling time

INGREDIENTS

For the panna cotta

500ml fresh double cream

315ml soya milk, unsweetened

180g caster sugar

1 tsp vanilla essence

4 sheets gelatine leaves

For the coulis

200g raspberries, fresh or frozen

1 tbsp icing sugar

Serve

Raspberry coulis

Fresh raspberries

Sprig of mint

I was inspired to create a panna cotta recipe with an Asian twist. One of my favourite street food desserts from Singapore is soya bean curd. I love the silken texture that soya milk brings. To give panna cotta an Asian twist, I had fun playing with the proportions and ingredients. Milk was replaced by soya milk in this recipe. The switch made the panna cotta much lighter, gave it a cleaner mouth feel and I was rewarded with a beautiful sexy wobble when the panna cotta was turned out! This is a really simple throw-everything-in-a-pan sort of recipe. I hope you will enjoy making, and eating it.

METHOD

1. **Make panna cotta:** Place all the ingredients for the panna cotta, except the gelatine leaves, in a saucepan. Bring to a gentle boil and stir until the sugar has dissolved.

2. In the meantime, soak the gelatine leaves in cold tap water for 1 minute until it is soft. Squeeze the water from the leaves and add them to the pan.

3. Remove the pan from the heat and stir until the gelatine leaves are thoroughly melted.

4. Cool the mixture, give it another stir and strain through a fine sieve into 6 ramekins. Chill overnight or for at least 4 hours.

5. **Make coulis:** Mash the fresh or thawed raspberries with the icing sugar, push through a sieve to remove the seeds.

6. **Unmold:** Dip the ramekin in a bowl of hot water for a mere second, turn the ramekin upside down, give it a gentle shake and the panna cotta should turn out. Place on a plate.

7. **Serve:** With the raspberry coulis, fresh raspberries and garnish with a sprig of mint.

CHEF'S TIPS

1. Gelatine leaf loses some of its setting properties when they are boiled.
2. Adjust the amount of icing sugar according to the sweetness of the raspberries and to your personal taste.

LILIAN'S SINGAPORE SLING

Serves: 1

Prep time: 5 minutes

INGREDIENTS

Ice

15ml fresh lime juice
(roughly half a lime)

30ml gin

15ml cherry brandy

7ml Cointreau

7ml Dom benedictine

10ml grenadine syrup

120ml pineapple juice

2 dashes Angostura
bitters

Garnish (optional)

Cherry

Pineapple wedge

Equipment

Measuring jigger

Cocktail shaker,
or jam jar with a lid

Tumbler glass

Straw

Following the turn of the century in colonial Singapore, Raffles Hotel was the gathering place for the expat community, and Long Bar was the watering hole. It was common to see gentlemen nursing glasses of gin or whisky, but etiquette dictated that the ladies were not allowed to consume alcohol in public!

Ngiam Tong Boon, who was working as a bartender at Long Bar, created a drink to keep his lady guests happy. An innocent looking fruit juice with a pink hue (a socially acceptable drink for women then), but he secretly packed it full of clear alcohol... ta da... presenting the birth of the Singapore Sling; by clever bartender Ngiam, in 1915!

METHOD

1. Put a large scoop of ice into a cocktail shaker (or jam jar).

2. Roll the limes on the work surface so that they release their juice more easily when squeezed. Use a teaspoon to scrap out the lime segments and add them to the shaker.

3. Measure and add the rest of the ingredients to the shaker, cover securely and shake well.

4. Pour into the glass, garnish as desired and serve with a straw.

CHEF'S TIPS

If serving a crowd, multiply the ingredients and store in a jug. Refresh the cocktail by shaking individually from this 'pre-mix' as needed, or use an electric blender if you are serving a few portions at a time.

"When we go on holiday we eat the best cuisine available, from street food to top restaurants. We just returned from Vietnam and Cambodia before attending Lilian's class. Her food tasted fantastic and some dishes even nicer then our holiday food! Despite using ingredients purchased in the UK, the taste was so authentic. I was that impressed I booked a place on the Street Food Class whilst eating the Thai and Vietnamese food we prepared!"
- Adrian Firth, Independent Financial Adviser

"Superb evening you created for Jane's birthday! She is still reeling from the surprise. All the family thank you for an absolutely fabulous experience. The cocktails, dim sum masterclass, stories and amazing food made it a remarkable and memorable experience. How will I ever top this? You left the kitchen in a much better state than when you arrived - truly amazing. A pleasure to meet you and thank you for sharing our special evening."
- Alan and Jane Clark

"Lilian is a fantastic teacher, her energy and enthusiasm is infectious. Her knowledge of ingredients, flavours and techniques are brilliant and she also has many handy time-saving tips for you to use in your kitchen at home! Definitely worth a day spent with Lilian if you want to expand your world food knowledge. Lilian is one of our guest chef, she teaches regular classes at the school and shares her incredible knowledge with our guests."
- Emily Mcveigh, General Manager, Kenton Hall Estate, The Food Hub Cookery School

"Lilian's food blows our minds! Authentic Asian cuisine of the highest standard, delivered with first class customer service too. I've used Lilian as a private chef for three celebratory events and each time she has overwhelmed us with terrific menus that is so delicious we hope for it to repeated often. Her excellent team work efficiently and unobtrusively at parties and I cannot recommend Lilian highly enough."
- Emma Lloyd, MD, We Are Relish Ltd

"My daughter and I had a wonderful time with Lilian. We had a very warm welcome, drinks and met the other participants, learned to sharpen knives and carved flowers from vegetables. We also prepared dumplings, chicken satay etc., all very enlightening, down to choosing ingredients! The dining table was set with amazing attention to detail, including refreshing lemongrass fragrance! We all sat down together to enjoy the fruits of our labour, so delicious!"
– Juliet Woods, Postmistress, Moreton Hall Post Office

"Your exceptional Chinese cookery class gave me so many tips that I'll be using for the rest of my days and recipes I will be recreating again and again. I had such a great time, thank you Lilian. I told you that my wok was the most unused item in my kitchen and you promised you would change that, and you certainly have… simply amazing."
– Kevin Hurst, Reporter at Bury Free Press

"Lilian takes us on wonderful taste journeys. We get transported through Asia in our living room! Every mouthful was incredible from the first to the last with each course more exciting than the last. Anything from her is always a complete sensory experience with tastes, smells, textures and visuals. She did private dinners and lesson in our home. We also went to her "Live Theatre Dining Experience". Lilian is a sensational chef with unforgettable food."
– Lisa & Maxine Vaughan

"We hired Lilian for the London Marathon party at Tower Bridge. We had 80 guests and she really hosted the party and pampered our guests very well. It was an Asian fusion theme, and all our family and friends were really amazed by how good she was. It will be a great pleasure to host another party with Lilian. Lilian you are the best!"
– Sadhna & Paresh Patel, MD, PES Limited

GIVING
THANKS

I have so many people to thank from the bottom of my heart and I thank God for the blessings in my life!

I would like to start by thanking my youngest sister Doris Hiw, who has done such a brilliant job of designing the cookbook and inspired me to do my very best. Thank you my darling little sister!

It is wonderful indeed to get offers of help. Adam Fennelow, despite your very busy schedule, you offered to edit my book. I am beyond touched. Thank you!

Emma Merton, you're so patient and kind. Nothing is too much trouble, taking things in your stride. I am forever grateful and appreciate your creativity and huge contribution to the book being published!

To Will Curtis, who so kindly and generously offered to store my cookbooks at his warehouse.

I am in awe of all my precious friends who have been testing the recipes. I want you to know that you have been my cheer leaders! You have been so encouraging along the process and I appreciate every single one of you walking this exciting journey with me.

- Andrew King
- Bruce Berry
- Claire Evans
- Jan Wade
- Lesley Graham
- Sophie Grover
- Warren Caulder
- Andrew Whitfield
- Chris Walling
- Hannah Cowling
- Jane Cappleman
- Lucy Bennett
- Valda Fisher

The hours of keeping house, cooking, laundry, running around and the continuous supply of tea while I was focusing on getting every page publication ready. You make my heart swell; I love you both very much! Jon Robinson & Daniel Robinson.

Thank you for the very generous sharing of your knowledge and expertise from the many cookbooks that you have written; and for the many links, connections and directions you have put my way. You are a pure and beautiful gem. I am very grateful indeed and so pleased that our paths crossed. Thank you so very much, Dawn Stock!

You hear my visions and support what I do, thank you for your contributions.
- Annie Hafermann
- Danny Lau
- Karen Cannard
- Angela Walling
- Jessie Lau
- Mike Merton

You guys are amazing!

For the countless hours of brainstorming, unconditional love, and support, putting me first before yourself. Always being there within a heartbeat, you have constantly been in the background since Lilian's Kitchen was born, holding my hand. You are my rock, Nancy Hiw!

You have always been there in every way, trustworthy and reliable. Thank you for your wise counsel and love, my most cherished big sister, Rina Hiw!

Food & prop styling LILIAN HIW
Food photography LILIAN HIW
Portrait photography TOM SOPER

Editor ADAM FENNELOW
Design & art direction DORIS HIW @ HIWDESIGN
Graphic designer EMMA MERTON

Print Management by Biddles Books Limited
First published 2024

ISBN: 978-1-916838-45-1

SCAN HERE
to visit my website
lilianskitchen.co.uk